Standard Grade Spanish
Course Notes

Maureen Andrew and Chris Dixon

Leckie×Leckie
Scotland's leading educational publishers

05/010708

Published by
Leckie & Leckie Ltd, 3rd Floor, 4 Queen Street, Edinburgh, EH2 1JE
tel: 0131 220 6831 fax: 0131 225 9987
enquiries@leckieandleckie.co.uk www.leckieandleckie.co.uk

Edited by Anna Sheppard and Lynda Swankie

Special thanks to
Andrea Collington (project management and page make-up),
Anna Sheppard (project management), BRW (creative packaging), Pumpkin House (concept design), Charlotte Rougvie (illustration), Caleb Rutherford (cover design), Phil Booth (sound engineering), Antonio Angel Pérez López, Kerry MacKinnon, Colin Meikle and Carla Sazunic (Spanish speakers)

ISBN 978-1-84372-145-1

A CIP Catalogue record for this book is available from the British Library.

® Leckie & Leckie is a registered trademark.

Leckie & Leckie is a division of Huveaux plc.

Acknowledgements

Leckie & Leckie is grateful to the copyright holders, as credited, for permission to use their material:

The Scottish Qualifications Authority for permission to reproduce past examination questions. (Answers do not emanate from the SQA.)

Faunia for permission to reproduce a leaflet (page 80).

Every effort has been made to trace the copyright holders and to obtain their permission for the use of copyright material. Leckie & Leckie will gladly receive information enabling them to rectify any error or omission in subsequent editions.

Contents

Contents

Introduction

Introduction

Welcome to Leckie and Leckie's Course Notes for Standard Grade Spanish!

Why learn Spanish?

A knowledge of a modern foreign language is a very useful skill in today's world. It can help you get more out of your holidays and improve your chances of getting a better job when you leave school – to say nothing of all the new people that it will give you the opportunity to talk to!

In these respects, Spanish is a very good language to learn. More and more Scots go to Spain on holiday every year, and Spanish is also one of the official languages of the European Union – which makes it very good for helping your job prospects. Spanish is spoken in almost all of South and Central America and is on the increase in the United States too. In fact, it is the third most widely spoken language in the world.

About these Course Notes

The aim of these Course Notes and the accompanying CD is to help you get the most out of your Standard Grade Spanish Course by letting you:

- familiarise yourself with the elements of Standard Grade Spanish
- develop and practise all the necessary skills
- organise your work throughout the course
- prepare your folio of Writing
- carry out your Speaking tests
- revise effectively for the exam

We have covered the most important aspects of the course in these Notes and CD and we hope that you will find using them an enjoyable experience. They will help you get the most out of learning Spanish – and get the best grade that you can for your final exams!

Skills assessed in Standard Grade Spanish

The four skills of Listening, Speaking, Reading, and Writing are all assessed for Standard Grade Spanish, but in calculating the overall grade more importance is given to Speaking and Reading. The Course Notes cover all of these skills, but more emphasis is put on the two skills which carry most weight.

The Course Notes are divided into the following sections:

Listening

- how to concentrate on key question words
- vocabulary and hints on extending yours (including a list of the most commonly occurring words from recent past papers)
- numbers
- hints for doing well in the Listening exam
- exercises based on the Listening exam

Speaking

- the three types of Speaking test are explained
- preparation and practice for the Presentation
- preparation and practice for the Role-play
- practice for the Conversation
- model answers for Speaking tests (also recorded for you to listen to on the CD)
- hints for doing well in your spoken Spanish

Reading

- advice on how to tackle the Reading exam
- examples of Foundation, General and Credit Reading from past papers
- original reading material for each level in Standard Grade, derived from Spanish publications
- hints for doing well in the Reading exam

Writing

- the folio of Writing
- how to make your Writing in Spanish effective
- examples of Writing tasks at Foundation, General and Credit level
- key phrases for improving your Writing
- hints for doing well in your folio of Writing

Grammar

- nouns and articles
- adjectives
- pronouns
  subject pronouns
  strong pronouns
  direct object pronouns
  indirect object pronouns
- verbs
  present tense
  reflexive
  radical changing
  irregular
  future
  conditional

imperfect

simple past

perfect and pluperfect

commands and the subjunctive

- prepositions

constructions with the infinitive

- grammar exercises

The CD

The accompanying CD is designed to help you develop your Speaking and Listening skills. It is divided into a number of sections. Each section helps you in a different way. For example, sometimes you will practise your Listening skills by listening to Spanish on the CD and answering questions printed in the Course Notes. At other times, you will practise your Speaking skills by listening carefully to Spanish phrases on the CD and then repeating them aloud as you hear each one. Follow the instructions at the start of each section of the CD. They tell you what to do in each section.

When you see the CD symbol in the book, be ready to listen to the CD.

Listen carefully to each section several times. This will help you do well in your Standard Grade Speaking tests and Listening exam.

All of the Listening material on the CD is spoken by native Spanish speakers. Some of the Speaking materials are spoken by Scottish students to make them realistic.

Exercises

Throughout the Course Notes there are exercises to help you practise what you have learnt.

When you see the exercise symbol in the Course Notes, be ready to do an exercise. Some of the exercises are designed to be done right away to help you practise what you have learned. Other exercises are designed to be done throughout your Standard Grade Spanish course.

Answers and transcripts

Where appropriate, you will find answers to exercises (and transcripts of exercises on the CD) at the end of each section.

Section 1: Listening

A guide to the Listening section of the exam

Key words

If you like *The Simpsons* (and let's face it, who doesn't?) you'll probably remember the episode in which Bart has to teach his dog, Santa's Little Helper, to be obedient. They both try really hard but the dog cannot understand a word Bart says. Finally, when it looks as if Santa's Little Helper is going to be taken away, he manages to pick out the single word 'Sit!' This is followed by 'Stay!' and 'Roll over!' The dog doesn't understand anything else but those few words are enough to get him through his obedience test.

Now no-one would suggest that a vocabulary of four words will get you an award in a Standard Grade Spanish exam but **by understanding key words you eliminate the need to know every word you hear**. This is also very important when you are trying to have a conversation.

Questions written in English

You should also remember that the questions you will be asked will be in English and they will be written on the exam paper. **The questions themselves will guide you to the parts of the Spanish that you need to concentrate on.** You will hear the Spanish three times, which should also give you plenty of opportunities to focus on the parts of the text you want.

The 'scenario' – your first clues

At the top of your question paper and at the start of the tape or CD you will hear what is called 'the scenario'. This is the setting or background against which the speaking on the tape is set. You might find, for example, that the scenario is that you are travelling to Spain or listening to a tape sent from a Spanish school. You should **listen carefully to the description of this scenario. It will give you your first clues to the answers** you should be looking for.

Number of marks = number of points

Check carefully how many marks are given for each question and **then try to find the same number of points for your answer** as you listen. However, do not write more than you need to – it may cost you marks. (Look at the *Pistas* for Reading on page 58.)

Listen, then write

Try not to write too much while the tape is playing. You may miss one answer while writing down another and, after all, there is time between the three playings for you to complete your answers.

Make an attempt

Do not leave blanks. **Make a <u>sensible</u> guess** if you have to.

Question types

Whatever the setting for your listening tests and whichever level you are sitting, the questions you are asked will belong to the following groups:

Where?   When?   Why?   What?   Who?   How?   How much/many?

Try these exercises to help you practise each of the areas in turn. After completing each exercise, check your answers. Once you have done this, read the transcript and replace the underlined phrases with other answers of your own. (NB. Look for the note by each exercise that directs you to the correct CD section and page for the transcript.)

Ejercicio 1   ¿Dónde?

Listen to the five sentences in Spanish that ask you to concentrate on **places** and answer these questions. Before trying the exercise make sure you have revised the words for different countries, places in the town and rooms in the house. Check that you know vocabulary such as 'beside', 'in front of', 'behind', etc.

TRACK 1

PAGE 28

No. QUESTION	MARKS
1. Where does this person live?	(2)
2. Where does this person spend her free time?	(2)
3. Where does this person's sister work?	(1)
4. Where will this person be spending the weekend?	(1)
5. Where will you meet up with your friend?	(1)

Now check the answers. Then read the transcript and replace the underlined phrases with other answers of your own.

Ejercicio 2   ¿Cuándo?

Now listen for **times, dates** or **seasons**. Do you know all the days of the week, months and seasons of the year in Spanish? Make sure you do before you start the exercise.

TRACK 2

PAGE 28

No. QUESTION	MARKS
1. When did this person visit Scotland?	(1)
2. How long did he spend there?	(1)
3. When does this person play basketball?	(2)
4. When is this person's birthday?	(1)
5. When is this person going to the United States?	(1)

Now check the answers. Then read the transcript and replace the underlined phrases with other answers of your own.

TRACK 3

PAGE 28

Ejercicio 3 ¿Por qué?

This time listen to the **reasons** people give.

No. QUESTION	MARKS
1. Why doesn't this girl want to go out tonight?	(1)
2. Why does this boy like English?	(2)
3. Why does this person like Spain?	(1)
4. Why can't this boy go to the cinema?	(1)
5. Why has the girl arrived late?	(1)

Now check the answers. Then read the transcript and replace the underlined phrases with other answers of your own.

TRACK 4

PAGE 29

Ejercicio 4 ¿Quién?

Now you should be listening for **people**. Before you begin, make a list of the Spanish words for all the family members you can. Do the same for as many jobs and professions as possible.

No. QUESTION	MARKS
1. Who is this person?	(1)
2. With whom is this person going on holiday?	(2)
3. Who is going to visit the town?	(1)
4. Who will be arriving tomorrow?	(1)
5. Who is going to the party?	(1)

TRACK 5

PAGE 29

Ejercicio 5 ¿Cómo?

This time listen for **how** things are done. Beforehand you might like to check how many methods of transport you can name.

No. QUESTION	MARKS
1. How does this person usually get to school?	(1)
2. How should you go about getting more information?	(1)
3. How does this person want his steak?	(2)
4. How would this person like to pay?	(1)
5. How should you complete the exercise?	(1)

Now check the answers. When you have done this read the transcript and replace the underlined phrases with other answers of your own.

Ejercicio 6 ¿Qué?

Listen to these five sentences to find **what** each person is talking about. Before doing the exercise revise the vocabulary for typical presents, food, sports, hobbies and classroom objects.

TRACK 6

PAGE 29

No.	QUESTION	MARKS
1.	What has this person lost?	(1)
2.	What birthday presents did this person receive?	(2)
3.	What is the boy's favourite food?	(1)
4.	What does this person do after school?	(1)
5.	What does this person want to know?	(1)

Now check the answers. Then read the transcript and replace the underlined phrases with other answers of your own.

Ejercicio 7 ¿Cuántos?

Finally listen for **how many**.

TRACK 7

PAGE 29

No.	QUESTION	MARKS
1.	How many pupils are in this person's class?	(1)
2.	How many children and grandchildren does this lady have?	(2)
3.	How many subjects does this girl study?	(1)
4.	How many rooms are in the house?	(1)
5.	How many times has this person been to France?	(1)

Now check the answers. Then read the transcript and replace the underlined phrases with other answers of your own.

El Vocabulario

When you are doing your listening exam you do not have a dictionary (you would not have enough time to look up words anyway) so it is really important that you learn as much vocabulary as possible beforehand.

To help you with this here is a selection of the words used in recent Standard Grade examinations. You should study this list very carefully while listening to your CD.

The words have been divided into sections to help you learn them. Each section is arranged alphabetically. Remember that words can be used in lots of different ways and could be found in more than one section.

TRACK 8

Mi familia y yo
- el marido
- mi hermana menor
- mi hermano mayor
- mi hijo/a
- mi mujer
- mi primo/a
- mi tío/a
- mis abuelos
- mis nietos
- mis padres

My family and I
the husband
my little sister
my big brother
my son/daughter
my wife
my cousin
my uncle/aunt
my grandparents
my grandchildren
my parents

TRACK 9

La casa y el hogar
- cómodo
- el comedor
- el cuarto de baño
- el cuarto de estar
- el dormitorio
- el jardín
- el salón
- el suelo
- la cocina
- la dirección
- la habitación
- la planta baja
- la primera planta
- la terraza

House and home
comfortable
the dining room
the bathroom
the living room
the bedroom
the garden
the lounge
the ground/the floor
the kitchen/cooking
the address
the room/bedroom
the ground floor
the first floor
the terrace

El colegio

- aprender
- difícil
- el alemán
- el dibujo
- el director
- el francés
- el hogar
- el inglés
- el profesor/la profesora
- fácil
- la biología
- la geografía
- la informática
- los alumnos
- los compañeros de clase
- un idioma
- un ordenador
- una asignatura
- una cinta

School

to learn
difficult
German
Art
the head teacher
French
Home Economics
English
the teacher
easy
Biology
Geography
IT
the pupils
the classmates
a language
a computer
a subject
a tape

TRACK 10

El tiempo de ocio

- dar un paseo
- deportista
- el alpinismo
- el baloncesto
- el billar
- el cine
- el deporte
- el periódico
- el polideportivo
- la bolera
- las noticias
- leer

Free Time

to go for a walk
sporty
climbing
basketball
billiards
the cinema
sport
the newspaper
sports centre
the bowling alley
the news
to read

TRACK 11

- libre — *free*
- los dibujos animados — *cartoons*
- mis ratos libres — *my free time*
- nadar — *to swim*
- quedarse en casa — *to stay at home*
- un baile — *a dance*
- un documental — *a documentary*
- un equipo — *a team*
- un partido — *a match*
- una canción — *a song*
- una entrada — *a ticket*
- una medalla de oro — *a gold medal*
- una película — *a film*
- una piscina — *a swimming pool*
- una revista — *a magazine*
- una sala de juegos — *a games room*

Las Mascotas — Pets

TRACK 12

- peces tropicales — *tropical fish*
- un gato — *a cat*
- un pájaro — *a bird*
- un perro — *a dog*
- una jaula — *a cage*

La Ropa — Clothes

TRACK 13

- las gafas de sol — *sun glasses*
- los zapatos de deporte — *trainers*
- los zapatos — *shoes*
- un jersey — *a jumper*
- un sombrero — *a hat*
- una camiseta — *a T-shirt*
- una chaqueta — *a jacket*
- una falda — *a skirt*
- una gorra — *a cap*
- unos calcetines — *socks*
- unos guantes — *gloves*
- unos pantalones — *trousers*
- unos vaqueros — *jeans*
- verde oscuro — *dark green*

Comer y Beber

- caliente
- el almuerzo
- el arroz
- el desayuno
- el helado
- el pan
- el pescado
- el pollo
- fresa
- frío
- la bebida
- la cena
- la comida
- los caramelos
- melocotón en almíbar
- platos típicos
- sabroso
- un bocadillo
- un huevo
- una copa
- vainilla

Food and Drink

hot

lunch

rice

breakfast

ice cream

bread

fish

chicken

strawberry

cold

drink

dinner

food/meal

sweets

peach in syrup

typical dishes

tasty

a sandwich

an egg

a glass

vanilla

TRACK 14

La Gente

- alto
- casarse
- conocer
- el cumpleaños
- herido
- la cara
- los bomberos
- moreno
- mucha gente
- regalar
- rubio
- ruso
- simpático
- un acento extranjero
- una enfermera
- viejo

People

tall

to get married

to know

birthday

hurt

face

the fire brigade

dark

lots of people

to give as a present

blond/fair

Russian

nice

a foreign accent

a nurse

old

TRACK 15

Hora/Fecha/Números

- ¿cuánto tiempo?
- a finales de
- a una hora fija
- a veces
- anoche
- antes de
- cada año
- cada día
- desde ... hasta
- después de
- el año pasado
- el año que viene
- en seguida
- esta noche
- este año
- estos días
- hace tres años
- hoy
- la primera vez
- la semana que viene
- mañana
- nunca
- otra vez
- siempre
- todas las noches
- todavía
- un mes
- un par de días

Times/Dates/Numbers

- *How long?*
- *at the end of*
- *at a fixed time*
- *sometimes*
- *last night*
- *before*
- *every year*
- *every day*
- *from ... till*
- *after*
- *last year*
- *next year*
- *immediately*
- *tonight*
- *this year*
- *these days*
- *three years ago*
- *today*
- *the first time*
- *next week*
- *tomorrow*
- *never*
- *again*
- *always*
- *every night*
- *still*
- *a month*
- *a couple of days*

Las Vacaciones

- descansar
- el albergue
- en el extranjero
- estar de vacaciones
- la playa
- la recepción
- tomar el sol
- un crucero
- un intercambio
- un país
- un recuerdo
- una muñeca

Holidays

- *to rest*
- *the inn*
- *abroad*
- *to be on holiday*
- *beach*
- *reception*
- *to sunbathe*
- *a cruise*
- *an exchange*
- *a country*
- *a souvenir*
- *a doll*

Viajar

- ¿Qué tal el viaje?
- a la derecha
- a la izquierda
- el asiento
- el mundo
- el último tren
- en barco
- llegar
- todo recto
- un atasco
- un autocar
- un aviso
- un billete
- un camión
- un choque
- un conductor
- un retraso
- una huelga
- viajar

Travel

How was the trip?
to the right
to the left
the seat
the world
the last train
by boat
to arrive
straight on
a traffic jam
a coach
an announcement
a ticket
a lorry
a collision
a driver
a delay
a strike
to travel

TRACK 18

El Trabajo y El Dinero

- alquilar
- bajar
- barato
- caro
- cheques de viaje
- gastar
- gratis
- libras esterlinas
- más o menos
- perder
- subir
- tarjetas de crédito
- una cartera

Work and Money

to hire/rent
to go down
cheap
dear
travellers' cheques
to spend
free
pounds
more or less
to lose
to go up
credit cards
a wallet

TRACK 19

TRACK 20

Ir de Compras

- abierto
- cerrado
- el mercado
- encontrar
- la sección de juguetes
- las flores
- las rebajas
- las tiendas
- los precios
- se abren
- se cierran
- un descuento
- un regalo
- una oferta especial
- unas toallas

To Go Shopping

open
closed
the market
to find
the toy department
flowers
sales
the shops
prices
they open
they close
a discount
a present
a special offer
towels

TRACK 21

Los Sentimientos

- ¡Qué suerte tenéis!
- ¿Quieres ...?
- aburrirse
- aguantar
- cansado
- Es mejor.
- Es una pena.
- Estoy harta.
- lo peor
- Lo siento mucho.
- Me encanta ...
- No me gusta nada.
- No se puede ...
- Tengo ganas de ...
- Tienes razón.

Feelings

How lucky you are!
Do you want ...?
to be bored
to put up with
tired
It's better.
It's a pity.
I am fed up.
the worst thing
I am very sorry.
I love ...
I don't like it at all.
You cannot ...
I want to ...
You are right.

TRACK 22

Los Lugares

- al lado de
- el ayuntamiento
- el paisaje
- el parque de atracciones
- el puerto
- la plaza de toros
- la plaza mayor
- lejos
- los lagos
- precioso

Places

beside
the town hall
the countryside
the funfair
the port
the bullring
the main square
far
the lakes
beautiful

- sitios de interés — *places of interest*
- un barrio — *a district*
- un castillo — *a castle*
- una biblioteca — *a library*
- una fábrica — *a factory*

El Tiempo / The Weather

TRACK 23

- buen tiempo — *good weather*
- el viento — *the wind*
- Hace calor. — *It's hot.*
- Hace frío. — *It's cold.*
- Hay niebla. — *It's foggy.*
- la lluvia — *the rain*
- Llueve. — *It's raining.*
- mal tiempo — *bad weather*
- una tormenta — *a storm*

La Rutina Diaria / Daily Routine

TRACK 24

- Come. — *He/she eats.*
- lavar el coche — *to wash the car*
- lavar los platos — *to do the dishes*
- limpiar — *to clean*
- Pasa la aspiradora. — *He/she does the hoovering.*
- Se levanta. — *He/she gets up.*

As well as these there are a few words that do not necessarily fit neatly into any of these categories

TRACK 25

- ¿Vale? — *OK?*
- a propósito — *by the way*
- a ver — *let's see*
- además — *furthermore*
- así que — *so that*
- bienvenidos — *welcome*
- claro — *of course*
- entre — *between*
- la pierna — *the leg*
- llamar — *to phone/call*
- resbalarse — *to slip*
- Se ha roto ... — *He/she has broken ...*
- sin — *without*
- sobre — *about*
- un incendio — *a fire*
- una cosa más — *one more thing*
- Ya lo sé. — *I know.*

'Seeing is hearing!'

There is no list of vocabulary that will include every word in your listening, especially at Credit Level. Try to concentrate, learn as much as you can before the exam and use your common sense. Remember that you will hear each item three times. If there is a word you can't get try to picture what it looks like. If you can do this 'seeing' is hearing!

This is not as difficult as it may at first sound. Think of the vowel sounds in Spanish – unlike our own language the pronunciation of them does not change. It is therefore relatively simple to identify them when you hear them. Additionally the sound we think of as 'th' will be written as either 'c' or 'z' in Spanish. Remember, too, that our 'ch' (as in loch) is the Spanish 'j' and the sound we hear as 'b' can be either 'b' or 'v'.

Listen to the CD. You will hear a list of words that are easier to understand in written form than when you listen to them. Take some time to picture what each one looks like, write it down (in Spanish!) and then work out the meaning.

When you have done this you can check your spelling and the meaning of each word from the transcript. You might also like to think of more examples of your own or make a note of any that you come across during your studies.

TRACK 26

PAGE 30

'Amigos falsos'

There are some words which do not mean what you might think. These are known as 'false friends' or 'amigos falsos'. Try to learn as many of these as possible so that you do not get caught out. Make a note of each one as you come across it. Here are a few to get you started:

- a finales de ...   *at the end of ...*
- actual   *present (i.e. at the moment)*
- largo   *long*
- constipado   *suffering from a cold*
- asistir   *to attend*
- pretender   *to claim*
- el campo   *the country*
- sensible   *sensitive*

You should also be careful with words like

- coche   *car*
- autocar   *coach*
- cómoda   *comfortable/chest of drawers*
- pensión   *boarding-house/pension*
- ganado   *won/earned/cattle*

> **Pista** Tip
>
> - As you work through your Standard Grade course you should note words like these which either do not mean what you might think at first or which might have more than one meaning.

Los Números

You can be certain that somewhere in your listening exam you will be asked at least one question based on numbers. It might be about someone's age, someone's family, a time, a date or the price of something. (Now that Spain has converted to euros prices can seem much more difficult.)

Ejercicio 1

Listen to the numbers 1–20 on the CD. You should then try to repeat each one to get used to the pronunciation. When you have done this several times you can check the transcript to make sure of the spelling.

TRACK 27

PAGE 31

Ejercicio 2

Listen to these ten sentences and write down the number mentioned in each one.

Now check your answers. Re-write each sentence, changing the number to one of your own.

TRACK 28

PAGE 31

Ejercicio 3

Listen to the numbers 21–50 on the CD. Practise saying them, then check the transcript as in Ejercicio 1.

TRACK 29

PAGE 32

Ejercicio 4

Once again you will hear ten sentences in which a number is mentioned. Write down each one.

Now check your answers, read the transcript and re-write each sentence with a number of your choice.

TRACK 30

PAGE 32

Ejercicio 5

Now you will hear the numbers 60, 70, 80, 90, 100. Listen, repeat and check as before.

TRACK 31

PAGE 33

Ejercicio 6

Write down the numbers as you hear them. Now check your answers.

TRACK 32

PAGE 33

Ejercicio 7

Listen to these numbers on the CD, paying special attention to how each one is made up.

108, 245, 326, 487, 555, 603, 778, 864, 912, 1000

Repeat and check the transcript as before. Then make up sentences using each of these numbers.

TRACK 33

PAGE 33

Ejercicio 8

Now listen to these ten conversations in which the prices of various items are given in euros, paying particular attention to how prices in euros are said. To make the exercise a little more difficult write down what each person wants to buy as well as how much it will cost.

When you have done this check your answers. You should then read the transcript and write ten conversations of your own, replacing the items which have been underlined with some of your own.

TRACK 34

PAGE 34

TRACK 35

PAGE 34

Ejercicio 9

Finally look at the following numbers, which are known as **ordinal** numbers ('first' instead of 'one', 'second' instead of 'two', etc.)

- primer(o)   *first*
- segundo   *second*
- tercer(o)   *third*
- cuarto   *fourth*
- quinto   *fifth*
- sexto   *sixth*
- séptimo   *seventh*

Note that each of these is an adjective, which means that the ending will change. Listen to the examples on the CD, then check the transcript. Try to write five examples of your own.

Credit Level Listening Exam

If you have managed to work your way through the exercises so far, making notes and taking time to revise the vocabulary given, you are well on your way to being ready for Foundation and General Level Listening examinations. At Credit Level, however, you need to be able to do a little more.

The question words are the same, the type of information requested is very similar and the approaches, especially focusing in on the key words or visualising the words you hear, are identical.

On the other hand, you can expect to hear much more Spanish in each question and you may well be asked to answer more than one type of question at a time. Do not let yourself be put off by this! Remember the Pistas at the beginning of this section and stick to them!

Pista Tip

At Credit Level you can expect to hear a fair amount about special occasions or events and 'disasters' of various types. For this reason it would be a good idea to get a firm grasp of vocabulary relating to the following:

- birthdays
- family members
- loss, robbery
- police, firefighters
- accidents, traffic jams, breakdowns, methods of transport
- weddings, parties, festivals, presents
- sporting events and outings
- breakages (objects and body parts!)
- disruptions (strikes, missed buses, etc.)

It may take you a while to learn all these words but the improvement in your results will make your efforts worthwhile.

Credit Level Listening Exercises

Now listen to these examples and complete the questions. Remember that in the exam you will hear the Spanish three times so when you practise you may listen several times if you have to.

Ejemplo número uno

You are in Spain with your friend José Ramón.

a. He tells you about a visit to Scotland.

    (i)   How long did he spend there? (1)

    (ii) What did he particularly enjoy? (1)

TRACK 36
PAGE 35

b. He gives you his opinions about his time in Scotland. What does he say about

    (i)   the food? (2)

    (ii) the television? (1)

Ejemplo número dos

The teacher of one of your Spanish friends is talking to you.

a. She tells you a little about her school. Mention any **two** pieces of information she gives you. (2)

TRACK 37
PAGE 35

b. She asks you about your school. What does she want to know? Mention **two** things. (2)

Ejemplo número tres

You are staying in a hotel in Spain.

a. In the dining room you speak to the manager about his job

    (i)   What does he like about it? (2)

    (ii) What does he not like? (1)

TRACK 38
PAGE 35

b. At the front desk you hear another guest talking with the receptionist.

    (i)   What exactly is the woman's problem? (2)

    (ii) What solution does the receptionist offer? (1)

Ejemplo número cuatro

You are staying with your Spanish friend. You are listening to the radio.

a. You hear an interesting news item. What is it about? Mention any **three** details. (3)

TRACK 39
PAGE 35

b. Next you hear an item of sports news.

    (i)   What is happening on the fifteenth of May?   (2)

    (ii)   What is special about the choice of venue for this event?   (2)

TRACK 40

PAGE 35

Ejemplo número cinco

You are visiting a friend in Spain.

a. You accompany her on a shopping trip.

    (i)   What **two** things does she want to buy?   (2)

    (ii)   What does the shop-assistant say about each of the items?   (2)

b. As you approach another shop you are stopped by a policeman.

    (i)   What does he tell you?   (2)

    (ii)   Why is this necessary?   (2)

TRACK 41

PAGE 36

Ejemplo número seis

You and your friend are staying at a youth hostel in the north of Spain.

a. The warden speaks to you.

    (i)   What does he tell you about the surrounding area?   (2)

    (ii)   What advice does he give you? Mention any **two** things.   (2)

b. He goes on to tell you about a recent event.

    (i)   What happened?   (2)

    (ii)   What was the result of this?   (2)

TRACK 42

PAGE 36

Ejemplo número siete

You are on an exchange visit with a family in Alicante.

a. Your exchange partner's mother explains some activities they have planned for you.

    (i)   What will you be doing tomorrow?   (2)

    (ii)   What has been planned for the next day?   (1)

b. She goes on to tell you about a special occasion which is coming up soon.

    (i)   What is this occasion?   (1)

    (ii)   What plans have been made for it?   (2)

Ejemplo número ocho

You are staying with your Spanish relatives.

TRACK 43

PAGE 36

a. Your aunt has found an interesting item in the newspaper.

    (i) What is going to happen?   (2)

    (ii) What will be the results of this?   (2)

b. She reads out a news item.

    (i) What exactly happened?   (1)

    (ii) What did the witnesses say?   (3)

Ejemplo número nueve

You are travelling in Spain.

TRACK 44

PAGE 36

a. As you queue for a ticket in the railway station a young woman goes up to the window.

    (i) What does she ask for?   (1)

    (ii) What question does she ask?   (1)

b. As the train arrives in Santander you hear an announcement about some changes to the timetable.

    (i) What is happening today?   (3)

    (ii) What reason is given for this?   (1)

Ejemplo número diez

You are travelling home after some time spent in Spain.

TRACK 45

PAGE 36

a. In the taxi to the airport you hear an item of traffic news.

    (i) What problem has occurred?   (1)

    (II) What are the results of this? Mention **two** things.   (2)

b. In the airport you hear an announcement.

    (i) What exactly is it about?   (3)

    (ii) The passengers are asked to do something. What is it?   (3)

Now check your answers. Once you have done this you should read the transcript very carefully and make a note of any new words you come across. You will probably find that there are quite a few!

Answers and Transcripts

Exercise 1

Answers

1. an apartment in the city
2. at the cinema or the bowling alley
3. Germany
4. the country
5. in front of the church

Transcript for track 1

1. Vivo en <u>un apartamento</u> en <u>la ciudad</u>.
2. Cuando tengo tiempo me gusta ir <u>al cine</u> o <u>a la bolera</u>.
3. Mi hermana trabaja como médica en <u>Alemania</u>.
4. Oye, este fin de semana lo voy a pasar <u>en el campo</u> con mis primos.
5. ¡Hasta luego! Nos vemos a las cuatro <u>delante de la iglesia</u>.

Exercise 2

Answers

1. three years ago
2. fifteen days/a fortnight
3. every Wednesday and Friday
4. 26 March
5. during the winter

Transcript for track 2

1. Pues, <u>hace tres años</u> fui a Escocia con mi mujer.
2. Estuvimos allí <u>quince días</u>.
3. Suelo jugar al baloncesto <u>todos los miércoles y viernes</u>.
4. Mi cumpleaños es <u>el veintiséis de marzo</u>.
5. Pues, voy a estar en los Estados Unidos <u>durante los meses de invierno</u>.

Exercise 3

Answers

1. She doesn't feel well.
2. It's easy and the teacher is nice.
3. The people are very nice.
4. He has lots of homework.
5. She had to help her mother.

Transcript for track 3

1. Oye, no me apetece salir esta tarde. Es que <u>me siento un poco enferma</u>.
2. A mí me encanta el inglés. <u>Es muy fácil y la profesora es simpática</u>.
3. Me gusta mucho España porque <u>la gente es muy amable</u>.
4. Lo siento. No puedo ir al cine porque <u>tengo muchos deberes</u>.
5. No he podido llegar antes porque <u>he tenido que ayudar a mi madre</u>.

Exercise 4

Answers

1. new maths teacher
2. husband and two children
3. members of the British Royal family
4. my cousins
5. classmates

Transcript for track 4

1. Bueno, chicos, yo soy vuestra <u>nueva profesora de matemáticas</u>.

2. Pronto salgo de vacaciones con <u>mi marido y mis dos hijos</u>.

3. En el mes de octubre nos vienen a visitar <u>algunos miembros de la familia real británica</u>.

4. Pues, mira, mañana llegan <u>mis primos</u>.

5. Pero, mamá, que <u>todos mis compañeros de clase</u> van a ir a la fiesta.

Exercise 5

Answers

1. in dad's car

2. phone for information

3. well done and with chips

4. by credit card

5. very carefully

Transcript for track 5

1. Suelo ir al insti <u>en el coche de mi padre</u>.

2. Si quieres recibir más información sobre este asunto <u>llámanos por teléfono</u>.

3. Quiero el filete <u>muy hecho</u> y <u>con patatas fritas</u>.

4. Por favor ¿sería posible pagar <u>con tarjeta de crédito</u>?

5. Bueno, este ejercicio hay que hacerlo <u>con mucho cuidado</u>.

Exercise 6

Answers

1. house keys

2. a computer and some CDs

3. shellfish

4. goes to friend's house

5. who is the weakest link

Transcript for track 6

1. He perdido <u>las llaves de casa</u>.

2. Pues, el día de mi cumpleaños me regalaron <u>un ordenador</u> y <u>unos discos compactos</u>.

3. Mi comida favorita es <u>el marisco</u>.

4. Después de las clases suelo <u>ir a casa de mi amigo</u>.

5. ¡Sepamos <u>quién es el rival más débil</u>!

Exercise 7

Answers

1. 33

2. 4 children, 7 grandchildren

3. 8 subjects

4. 9 rooms

5. 4 times

Transcript for track 7

1. Me encanta el cole. En mi clase hay <u>treinta y tres</u> alumnos.

2. Tengo una familia numerosa con <u>cuatro hijos y siete nietos</u>.

3. Siempre tengo muchos deberes porque estudio <u>ocho asignaturas</u>.

4. Ahora te voy a enseñar la casa. Tiene <u>nueve habitaciones</u>.

5. Me encanta viajar. Ya he visitado Francia <u>cuatro veces</u>.

'Seeing is hearing!'

TRACK 26

• rival	*rival*
• jersey	*jumper, jersey*
• maravilloso	*marvellous*
• vídeo	*video*
• región	*region*
• teatro	*theatre*
• centro	*centre*
• inconveniente	*inconvenient*
• popularidad	*popularity*
• compañía	*company*
• ideal	*ideal*
• estación	*station*
• identificar	*to identify*
• prolongar	*to prolong*
• prohibido	*prohibited, forbidden*
• razonable	*reasonable*
• en general	*in general*

Los Números – Answers and Transcripts

Exercise 1

Transcript for track 27

uno o una

dos

tres

cuatro

cinco

seis

siete

ocho

nueve

diez

once

docc

trece

catorce

quince

dieciséis

diecisiete

dieciocho

diecinueve

veinte

Exercise 2

Answers

1. 6

2. 3

3. 17

4. 12

5. 8

6. 9

7. 2

8. 10

9. 13

10. 20

Transcript for track 28

1. Tengo seis hermanos.

2. Nuestros vecinos tienen tres coches.

3. Mi amigo tiene diecisiete años.

4. Voy a comprar doce lápices.

5. Salgo de casa a las ocho.

6. Estuvimos en España hace nueve meses.

7. Hay que hacer eso dos veces a la semana.

8. Llegaremos dentro de diez minutos.

9. Aquel edificio tiene trece pisos.

10. Mi camisa nueva me costó veinte libras esterlinas.

Exercise 3

Transcript for track 29

veintiuno

veintidós

veintitrés

veinticuatro

veinticinco

veintiséis

veintisiete

veintiocho

veintinueve

treinta

treinta y uno

treinta y dos

treinta y tres

treinta y cuatro

treinta y cinco

treinta y seis

treinta y siete

treinta y ocho

treinta y nueve

cuarenta

cuarenta y uno

cuarenta y dos

cuarenta y tres

cuarenta y cuatro

cuarenta y cinco

cuarenta y seis

cuarenta y siete

cuarenta y ocho

cuarenta y nueve

cincuenta

Exercise 4

Answers

1. 29
2. 42
3. 26
4. 37
5. 49
6. 35
7. 28
8. 47
9. 33
10. 41

Transcript for track 30

1. Mi cumpleaños es el día veintinueve de agosto.

2. Mi padre tiene cuarenta y dos años.

3. En mi clase de matemáticas hay veintiséis alumnos.

4. Mi dirección es Calle San Fernando treinta y siete.

5. Hay que coger el autobús número cuarenta y nueve.

6. Tenemos treinta y cinco días de vacaciones al año.

7. El pueblo está a veintiocho kilómetros de aquí.

8. Mi prima tiene una colección de cuarenta y siete muñecas.

9. La cafetería ofrece treinta y tres sabores de helado.

10. La carrera duró unos cuarenta y un segundos.

Exercise 5

Transcript for track 31

sesenta

setenta

ochenta

noventa

cien

Exercise 6

Answers

1. 64
2. 85
3. 99
4. 72
5. 81
6. 63
7. 94
8. 76
9. 67
10. 80

Transcript for track 32

sesenta y cuatro

ochenta y cinco

noventa y nueve

setenta y dos

ochenta y uno

sesenta y tres

noventa y cuatro

setenta y seis

sesenta y siete

ochenta

Exercise 7

Transcript for track 33

ciento ocho

doscientos cuarenta y cinco

trescientos veintiséis

cuatrocientos ochenta y siete

quinientos cincuenta y cinco

seiscientos tres

setecientos setenta y ocho

ochocientos sesenta y cuatro

novecientos doce

mil

Exercise 8

Answers

1.	two loaves	0·60 euros
2.	woollen socks	5·50 euros
3.	ham sandwich	2·20 euros
4.	tin of sardines	1·75 euros
5.	a kilo of sugar	0·86 euros
6.	two white coffees	3·40 euros
7.	a white T-shirt	15·60 euros
8.	a black pen, a ruler	1·90 euros
9.	a portion of omelette	4·10 euros
10.	a red wine, two orange juices	6·05 euros

Transcript for track 34

1. (a) Quisiera <u>dos barras de pan</u>, por favor.

   (b) Son sesenta céntimos.

2. (a) Quiero <u>unos calcetines de lana</u>, por favor

   (b) Son cinco con cincuenta euros.

3. (a) ¿Me da <u>un bocadillo de jamón</u>, por favor?

   (b) Muy bien, dos con veinte euros.

4. (a) ¿Cuánto vale <u>la lata de sardinas</u>, por favor?

   (b) Uno con setenta y cinco euros.

5. (a) ¿Me pone <u>un kilo de azúcar</u>, por favor?

   (b) En seguida. Ochenta y seis céntimos, por favor.

6. (a) <u>Dos cafés con leche</u>, por favor.

   (b) Muy bien. Tres con cuarenta euros.

7. (a) Busco <u>una camiseta blanca</u>.

   (b) Pues, ésta vale quince con sesenta euros.

8. (a) Quiero <u>un bolígrafo negro</u> y <u>una regla</u>.

   (b) Muy bien. Uno con noventa euros, por favor.

9. (a) Quisiera <u>una ración de tortilla</u>, por favor.

   (b) Bien. Cuatro con diez euros.

10. (a) <u>Un vino tinto</u> y <u>dos zumos de naranja</u>, por favor.

    (b) En seguida. Seis con cinco euros.

Exercise 9

Transcript for track 35

1. Vivimos en la primera planta del edificio.

2. Acabo de leer el segundo capítulo del libro.

3. Es la tercera vez que lo he visto.

4. La cuarta en terminar la carrera ha sido la española.

5. Hay que subir al quinto piso, séptima puerta.

Ejemplo número uno

a. Oye, ¿sabías que yo ya he visitado Escocia? Pues sí, pasé seis semanas en el este del país. Me gustó mucho Escocia y aprecié sobre todo los campos de golf. Me encanta este deporte.

TRACK 36

b. Lo siento mucho pero debo decirte que no me gustó nada la comida escocesa. Tiene mucha grasa y todo el mundo come patatas fritas todos los días. Pero, por otro lado, los programas de televisión son mucho mejores que en España. ¿Estás de acuerdo?

Ejemplo número dos

a. ¿Qué te parece nuestro instituto? Es el más grande de la ciudad, con casi mil setecientos alumnos. Y ¡fíjate! el inglés es obligatorio para todos.

TRACK 37

b. Bueno, quisiera saber algo de la vida escolar en tu país. ¿Cuántas asignaturas tenéis que estudiar? ¿Es cierto que todos tenéis que llevar uniforme?

Ejemplo número tres

a. Hace cinco años que trabajo en este hotel. Me encanta hablar con gente de otros países e intentar resolver sus problemas. Pero desafortunadamente tengo que trabajar muchas horas al día, lo que me fastidia bastante.

TRACK 38

b. –¡Oiga! ¿Me ayuda, por favor? Tengo un problema con mi habitación. Es que hace dos días que el agua de la ducha sale fría. ¡Ya estoy harta!
–¿Aún no ha venido el fontanero? Lo siento muchísimo. Ahora mismo lo voy a llamar otra vez.

Ejemplo número cuatro

a. Noticias de última hora. Según un portavoz, el Rey Don Juan Carlos ha sido trasladado al hospital de Nuestra Señora de la Gracia de Palma de Mallorca. Al parecer el rey se ha roto la pierna derecha mientras practicaba el esquí acuático. La Reina, Doña Sofía, ha acompañado a su marido al hospital.

TRACK 39

b. Y ahora algo de gran interés para los aficionados del fútbol. El partido amistoso entre la selección española y la de Inglaterra tendrá lugar el miércoles, quince de mayo. El partido se jugará en el Estadio Vicente Calderón en Madrid. Será la primera vez desde hace diez años que se juega un partido internacional allí.

Ejemplo número cinco

a. –Buenos días. Quisiera comprar un jersey en lana pura y una chaqueta impermeable.
–Muy bien, señorita. Los jerseys en lana los tenemos en todos los colores pero desafortunadamante no quedan chaquetas para mujeres. Sólo las tenemos para hombres.

TRACK 40

b. Un momento, chicos. Ahora no se puede entrar en la tienda. Se ha evacuado el edificio porque se ha descubierto un incendio en el departamento de electrodomésticos. ¿Por qué no volvéis más tarde?

TRACK 41

Ejemplo número seis

a. Bienvenidos a nuestro albergue. Ya sé que os vais a divertir mucho aquí. En esta región hay unas montañas preciosas pero debéis daros cuenta de que también pueden ser muy peligrosas. Hay que tener mucho cuidado así que si vais a hacer alpinismo llevad la ropa correcta y avisadme de la ruta que vais a seguir.

b. Hace unas semanas un grupo de turistas franceses se perdió en las montañas y nuestros voluntarios tuvieron que buscarlos durante casi dos días. No queremos en absoluto que se repita eso.

TRACK 42

Ejemplo número siete

a. Pues, hemos planeado muchas cosas para ti. Mañana pensamos llevarte a una playa muy bonita para nadar y tomar el sol y luego pasado mañana iremos a visitar algunos de los monumentos históricos de la región.

b. A propósito, dentro de unos días la abuela va a celebrar su cumpleaños. El martes cumplirá los ochenta años. Toda la familia va a venir aquí y vamos a organizar una fiesta sorpresa. ¡Qué bien nos lo vamos a pasar!

TRACK 43

Ejemplo número ocho

a. Bueno, aquí en el periódico pone que hay una huelga de autobuses la semana que viene. Habrá tantos coches en la carretera que tendremos que salir muy temprano para llegar al trabajo a tiempo.

b. ¡Fíjate! Ayer hubo un atraco en nuestro banco. Pues sí, a las diez de la mañana. Según los testigos los atracadores eran dos hombres y una mujer. Todos hablaban con un acento un poco raro y uno de los hombres llevaba una pistola. ¡Vaya susto que se llevaron los empleados!

TRACK 44

Ejemplo número nueve

a. ¡Buenas tardes! Quisiera un billete de ida y vuelta de segunda clase para Barcelona, por favor. A propósito, ¿hay algún descuento para los menores de dieciocho años?

b. ¡Atención! ¡Atención! Les avisamos que a partir de las veinte horas los trenes con destino al norte saldrán con una hora de retraso. Esto se debe a un problema eléctrico que estamos intentando solucionar. Perdonen las molestias.

TRACK 45

Ejemplo número diez

a. Tenemos un aviso para los conductores que se dirigen al aeropuerto por la Nacional Siete. Se ha producido un accidente entre dos autocares en esta carretera. A consecuencia de esto la carretera queda cerrada al tráfico y todos tendrán que seguir otra ruta.

b. Se ha perdido la niña Marta Aguirre Velázquez de cinco años. La niña es pequeña y rubia y lleva un vestido rojo. Por favor, en caso de que encuentren a la niña perdida llévenla directamente a la Oficina de Información situada en la planta baja de este edificio.

Ejemplo número uno

a. (i)   six weeks   (1)

   (ii) golf <u>courses</u>   (1)

b. (i)   greasy

      (everyone eats) chips
      every day   (2)

   (ii) much better than in Spain (1)

Ejemplo número dos

a. 2 from:
   – biggest in the city
   – <u>almost</u> 1700 pupils
   – all <u>must</u> study English   (2)

b. How many subjects do you
   (we) have to study?

   Does everyone have to wear
   uniform?   (2)

Ejemplo número tres

a. (i)   meeting people from
      other countries

      solving their problems   (2)

   (ii) the hours he has to work
      (every day)   (1)

b. (i)   for two days

      the water in the shower
      has been cold   (2)

   (ii) he will phone the
      plumber (again)   (1)

Ejemplo número cuatro

a. 3 from:
   – King Juan Carlos in hospital
   – has broken (right) leg
   – Done while water-skiing
   – Queen Sofía with him in the
     hospital   (3)

b. (i)   international <u>football</u>
      match

      Spain vs England   (2)

   (ii) first time for ten years

      the ground has been
      used for an international   (2)

Ejemplo número cinco

a. (i)   <u>wool</u> jumper

      rainproof jacket   (2)

   (ii) they have jumpers in all
      colours

      no rainjackets for women/
      only have rainjackets for
      men   (2)

b. (i)   cannot go into shop

      it has been evacuated   (2)

   (ii) small fire discovered

      in household appliances
      department   (2)

Ejemplo número seis

a.   (i)   beautiful mountains

but can also be very
dangerous   (2)

(ii)   wear correct clothes when
climbing

let him know route you
will be taking   (2)

b.   (i)   group of French tourists

lost in mountains   (2)

(ii)   volunteers had to search for
them

for <u>almost</u> two days   (2)

Ejemplo número siete

a.   (i)   visiting pretty beach

to swim <u>and</u> sunbathe   (2)

(ii)   visit historical monuments (1)

b.   (i)   granny's 80th birthday   (1)

(ii)   family all coming here

surprise party   (2)

Ejemplo número ocho

a.   (i)   bus strike

next week   (2)

(ii)   lots of traffic

need to leave early (to
get to work on time)   (2)

b.   (i)   bank robbery   (1)

(ii)   two men and one woman

strange accent

one man had gun   (3)

Ejemplo número nueve

a.   (i)   second class return to
Barcelona   (1)

(ii)   Any discount for under
eighteens?   (1)

b.   (i)   from 8pm

trains for the north

delayed for one hour   (3)

(ii)   electrical problem   (1)

Ejemplo número diez

a.   (i)   accident between two
coaches   (1)

(ii)   road closed

need to use another route (2)

b.   (i)   five year old girl lost

small and blonde

wearing red dress   (3)

(ii)   if they find her

take her to Information
Office

on ground floor   (3)

Section 2: Speaking

The Speaking section of the course

The sounds of Spanish and the alphabet

Useful words and phrases

Speaking test practice – prepared talks

Speaking tests – role-play

Speaking tests – general conversation

Transcripts

The Speaking section of the course

Speaking is a **very important** skill and is worth one third of the marks for Standard Grade Spanish.

During your Standard Grade course, you will have three different types of Speaking test:

- Prepared talk
- Role-play
- Conversation

Each of these is equally important. Your teacher will award you a grade from 1–6 for each of these activities and the final grade that you will get for Speaking will be the average of the three.

The sounds of Spanish and the alphabet

The pronunciation of Spanish is fairly straightforward and, as Spanish speakers can tell how a word is pronounced from the way it is spelled, they don't use the alphabet very much.

Pistas   Hints and Tips

- Don't try to learn the whole Spanish alphabet off by heart – you'll probably never need it. Just learn the letters you need to spell your name and address – those might sound odd to a Spanish speaker and you might be asked to spell them.

- When you see a Spanish word written down, you should pronounce most of the letters just the way you do in English – although Spanish speakers tend to pronounce the sounds more clearly than many English speakers. There are only a few letters that you need to pay special attention to. We have given you examples of how these are pronounced on the CD too.

Listening exercise 1

We have the Spanish alphabet on the CD for you. There are more 'letters' than in the English alphabet because Spanish traditionally regards, **'ch'**, **'ll'**, **'ñ'** and **'rr'** as separate letters.

The letter **'c'** can have three different sounds. It is most often pronounced like the **'c'** in cat in words like:

TRACK 46

PAGE 50

casa   tocar

When it is followed by the letter **'h'** it is pronounced just like **'ch'** in English:

chocolate con churros

But when it is followed by **'e'** or **'i'** it is pronounced like the **'th'** sound that you get at the end of an English word like 'with':

cielo   hacer

The letter 'z' in Spanish has this same **'th'** sound:

zorro   azul

Spanish also has a sound like the Scots' pronunciation of **'ch'** at the end of the word 'loch'. In Spanish this is called the **'jota'** sound. The letter **'j'** is always pronounced like this:

jardín   ojalá

The letter 'g' is also pronounced like this when it is followed by **'e'** or **'i'**:

gerente   agente

Double **'l'** is pronounced a bit like the sound in the middle of the English word 'million':

llamada   callar

Finally, the letter **'ñ'** – the **'n'** with a little mark called a 'tilde' over it – is pronounced a bit like the sound in the middle of the English word 'onion':

niño   año

Useful words and phrases

Listening exercise 2

This part of the CD contains useful words and phrases for a whole variety of situations in a Standard Grade Speaking test. Listen carefully and repeat the words and phrases over and over again. At first, try it with the book. As you gain more confidence you can try it without the book.

TRACK 47

Saying hello

¡Buenos días!	*Good morning*
¡Buenas tardes!	*Good afternoon/evening*
¡Hola!	*Hello*
¡Buenas!	*Hello*

Introductions

Éste es ...	*This is ... (introducing a man/boy)*
Ésta es ...	*This is ... (introducing a girl/woman)*
Te presento a ...	*This is ...*

Saying goodbye

¡Chao!	*Bye*
¡Adiós!	*Bye*
¡Hasta luego!	*See you soon*
¡Buenas noches!	*Good night*

Offering good wishes

¡Felicidades!	*Congratulations*
¡Feliz cumpleaños!	*Happy birthday*
¡Qué te vaya bien!	*All the best*
¡Feliz Navidad!	*Merry Christmas*
¡Próspero Año Nuevo!	*Happy New Year*

Attracting someone's attention

¡Perdone!	*Excuse me*
¡Oiga!	*Excuse me*
Señor	*Sir*
Señora	*Madam*
Señorita	*Miss*

Thanking people

Gracias	*Thank you*
Muchas gracias	*Thank you very much*

Apologising

Lo siento	*I'm sorry*
¡Perdóneme!	*I'm sorry*

Pista

In addition to learning to say these phrases, write them in a notebook to help you remember them. Don't forget to leave enough space under each heading to add examples you find during your course.

- ¡Discúlpame! — *I'm sorry*
- Lo siento mucho — *I'm very sorry*

Saying that you like something

- Me gusta el deporte. — *I like sport.*
- Me gusta bailar. — *I like dancing.*
- Me gustan las películas de miedo. — *I like horror films.*
- Me gusta mucho ver la televisión. — *I like watching television.*
- Me chifla estudiar. — *I love studying.*

TRACK 48

Saying that you don't like something

- No me gustan las verduras. — *I don't like vegetables.*
- No me gusta nada ir al teatro. — *I don't like going to the theatre at all.*
- No me gusta en absoluto leer. — *I don't like reading at all.*
- Me da asco la música clásica. — *I can't stand classical music.*
- Odio las arañas. — *I hate spiders.*

Saying you have no strong opinions about something

- Me da igual ir al colegio. — *Going to school doesn't bother me.*
- No me importa el béisbol. — *I'm not bothered about baseball.*
- No me interesan los videojuegos. — *I'm not interested in computer games.*

Agreeing

- ¡Vale! — *That's okay.*
- ¡Está bien! — *That's fine.*
- ¡Eso es! — *That's it.*
- ¡Perfecto! — *That'll do nicely.*
- Estoy de acuerdo. — *I agree.*
- Tienes razón. — *You're right.*

TRACK 49

Disagreeing

- ¡No me digas! — *You must be joking!*
- ¿Me estás tomando el pelo? — *Are you pulling my leg?*
- No estoy de acuerdo. — *I disagree.*
- No es el caso. — *That's not so.*
- No está bien. — *That's not good.*
- No vale nada. — *That's no good at all.*
- Te equivocas. — *You're wrong.*
- ¡En absoluto! — *No way!*

Accepting something you are offered

- Sí, gracias. — *Yes, thanks.*
- ¡Excelente! — *That's excellent.*
- ¡Qué guay! — *That's great.*
- ¡Fenomenal! — *That's great.*

TRACK 50

Refusing something you are offered

- No, gracias.   *No, thanks.*
- No me apetece.   *I don't fancy it.*

Saying what you'd like

- Quiero un vaso de leche, por favor.   *I'd like a glass of milk please.*
- Quiero dejar el colegio lo antes posible. *I want to leave school as soon as possible.*
- Una coca cola, por favor.   *A coke, please.*
- Me gustaría visitar *Terra Mítica*.   *I'd like to go to Terra Mítica.*
- ¿Me trae otra cuchara?   *Can you bring me another spoon?*

Asking for permission

- ¿Puedo ir al cine esta tarde?   *Can I go to the cinema this evening?*
- ¿Se puede dejar el bolso aquí?   *Can I leave my bag here?*
- ¿Es posible hablar con el gerente?   *May I speak with the manager?*

TRACK 51

Inviting someone to do something

- ¿Te gustaría tomar algo?   *Would you like a drink?*
- ¿Qué te parece si vamos al fútbol?   *Would you like to come to the football with me?*
- ¿Quieres dar un paseo por la playa?   *Would you like to go for a walk on the beach?*

Saying you have to do something

- Tengo que estudiar más en matemáticas.   *I have to work harder in maths.*
- Necesito dejar las llaves con mi padre.   *I have to leave the keys with my dad.*
- Debo ir a visitar a mi abuela.   *I must visit my gran.*

TRACK 52

Things to say to give yourself time to think

- Bueno ...   *Well ...*
- Pues ...   *Well ...*
- Mira ...   *Look ...*
- Es que ...   *It's just that ...*

Things to say when you are struggling with your Spanish

- No entiendo.   *I don't understand.*
- No comprendo.   *I don't understand.*
- ¿Quieres repetir, por favor?   *Could you say that again, please?*
- ¿Quieres hablar más despacio, por favor? *Could you speak more slowly, please?*
- Más despacio, por favor.   *Slower, please.*
- Más alto, por favor.   *Speak up, please.*
- ¿Hablas inglés?   *Do you speak English?*

Now, let's practise each of the three types of Standard Grade Speaking tests.

Speaking test practice – prepared talks

A lot of the language you use in a prepared talk may be useful in a Writing exercise, because you could be asked to speak **or** write about yourself, your hobbies, or a recent holiday or another subject.

Exercise 1 – Personal information prepared talk

Listen to the next section of the CD. In it Andrew gives a prepared talk in which he tells us a bit about himself. Let's look at what he says:

TRACK 53

PAGE 50

General level answer

Andrew begins by telling us his name, his age and where he lives. He then goes on to tell us a bit about his family.

> Me llamo Andrew. Tengo 15 años. Vivo en Dundee.
>
> En mi familia hay cuatro personas: mi madre, mi padre, mi hermana y yo. Mi madre se llama June y tiene 40 años. Ella es ama de casa. Mi padre se llama David y tiene 42 años. Él es fontanero. Mi hermana se llama Lyndsey y tiene 10 años. Ella está en la escuela primaria.

After that, he tells us about his school.

> En mi colegio hay 600 estudiantes y 40 profesores. Yo estudio ocho asignaturas. El inglés, las matemáticas, la historia, la química, la física, la música, la informática y el español.

Finally, he tells us something about his spare time:

> En mi tiempo libre me gusta escuchar música, jugar al futbol e ir a las discotecas el fin de semana.

What do you think about his prepared talk? His **pronunciation** is good, he follows a **clear structure** and gives a lot of **information**. His teacher agrees it's good and tells him he would probably be awarded a Grade 3, a good general level award.

Credit level answer

BUT if Andrew wants a **credit award**, he needs to do some more work on it. He is using very simple language, which he needs to develop further. Let's look at each section to see how he does this.

> Hola, me llamo Andrew. Tengo 15 años y vivo en una ciudad en el noreste de Escocia que se llama Dundee.

SECTION 2

Speaking

Just by saying hello, Andrew is **talking to you** rather than sounding as though he is just reading. **His sentences are longer**: he's using words like '**y**' and '**que**' to link together the things he was saying; he has added **more detail** by telling us more about where Dundee is. This all helps to make the language less simple.

How can he improve what he says about his family? Let's see.

> Bueno ... Somos cuatro personas en mi familia: mi padre, mi madre, mi hermana y yo. Mi madre, que se llama June, tiene 40 años y es ama de casa. Mi padre, David, tiene 42 años y es fontanero. Me llevo bastante bien con mis padres, pero mi padre es muy estricto. Por eso, me llevo mejor con mi madre. Mi hermana pequeña se llama Lyndsey. Tiene sólo 10 años y está todavía en la escuela primaria. No me llevo bien con ella. Hay siempre disputas en casa, sobre todo cuando yo quiero ver el fútbol en la televisión y ella no.

This is clearly much better, isn't it? He's done the same sort of things as he did with the first section, joining up short sentences into longer ones and giving more detail. He's using words like '**pero**' and '**por eso**' to **expand or explain things** and he's using words like '**sólo**', '**todavía**' and '**siempre**' to **give even more information**.

Let's see what he has to say about his school now.

> Voy a un colegio grande en el centro de la ciudad. En mi instituto hay más o menos 600 estudiantes y unos 40 profesores. Me gusta bastante el colegio porque tengo muchos amigos allí. Pero tengo mucho trabajo puesto que estudio ocho asignaturas. Las asignaturas que me gustan bastante son el inglés, la historia, la música y la informática. Las que no me gustan son las matemáticas, la química y la física. El español me da igual.

Again, there's more detail and he's combined his ideas into longer sentences. He has added interest by **telling us what he thinks** about his subjects, rather than just listing them.

What about his free time?

> Pues, con todo el trabajo que tengo que hacer por el colegio no tengo mucho tiempo libre. Cuando puedo, me gusta escuchar música y jugar al fútbol con mis compañeros. Pero lo que más me gusta es el fin de semana, cuando no hay colegio, salir a la discoteca con mi novia. Lo pasamos bomba.

Again he has used the same sorts of simple techniques to make his sentences longer and give more detail, making good use of words like '**pues**', '**pero**', and '**cuando**'.

Now listen to this second version of his talk on the CD. In fact, Andrew's talk is a bit longer than yours would need to be but it is very good. Well done, Andrew, this will get a credit award.

TRACK 54

PAGE 51

Practice in composing a prepared talk

Using the second version of Andrew's talk, change the personal details and opinions so that they are about you. Then you will be able to tell people what you think about your family, school and hobbies. You'll find useful phrases in the first section of this chapter to help you do this. You can also use a dictionary to find vocabulary.

Record your talk and listen to how you sound. That way you'll be able to find ways to improve. You could also try asking your teacher for help and advice.

Exercise 2 – Prepared talk about your town

Here are some of the key points to remember from Exercise 1:

- Prepare your talk well

- Plan how to structure it

- Show off your Spanish by giving more information.

Keeping these points in mind, prepare a talk for a group of Spanish students visiting your school about your hometown.

Before you start, think about the sort of things that will interest them, such as:

- A little about the history of your town

- Something about the weather

- Something about transport facilities

- Information about shopping

- Things to do like cinema, theatre, museums, sports, discos.

How to get the information in Spanish

If you live in a large town, your local tourist office may have information in Spanish. This can be a very quick way of getting the right vocabulary. If not, your course book or class work may focus on the theme of 'places of interest'. Here are a few useful words we've compiled to get you started. If you don't recognise any words, use your dictionary to find them and any other words you may need:

el castillo; el puerto; los grandes almacenes; el polideportivo; la piscina; el centro histórico; el centro comercial; el cine; el teatro; la discoteca; la calle; los autobuses; los trenes; la catedral; el museo

Once you've written down your talk and practised it, record it to see how you sound. You might like to try it out on your teacher or another Spanish speaker for their advice.

Then listen to the next section of the CD, in which a girl tells you about her hometown of Edinburgh. Is there anything in it that can help you improve your talk?

TRACK 55

PAGE 51

Speaking tests – role-play

The second type of speaking test is role-play. You might find this easier than a prepared talk, because you will be given much more detailed information about what you have to do.

Usually, you will be asked to play yourself. You'll be given an imaginary situation in which your teacher will play the person you will speak to.

Key points – preparing for role-play

- Look through some of the helpful words and phrases on pages 42–44 and pick out the ones that you might need.

- Make up a plan using some of the phrases you have chosen

- Note the facts you might want to include

- Be ready for the unexpected! Your partner may not say exactly what you expect and the conversation may not go exactly as you expect!

Exercise 3 – Role-play – Arranging to go to a football match

The scenario

Imagine that you will meet a Spanish pupil who is visiting your school on an exchange. You will ask her/him if she/he would like to go to a football match with you.

Preparation

1. Look through some of the helpful words and phrases on pages 42–44 and pick out the ones that you think you might need.

2. Next make up a plan using some of the phrases you have chosen.

3. Make a note of facts that you might want to include in your conversation – like where the game is, when it starts, where and when you should meet and how you will get there.

4. Look back at the question words on pages 11–13 of the Listening section and listen carefully to the appropriate part of the CD. That will help you to be ready for whatever questions you are asked by the person you are speaking to!

TRACK 56

Role-play

Now try out your role-play with a partner – a classmate, your teacher or another Spanish speaker.

TRACK 57

PAGES 52–53

Try listening to the version of this role-play on the CD. We have recorded this twice, once with both parts included and the second time with gaps for your part so you can try out your version of the dialogue with a recorded voice.

Exercise 4 – Role-play – Complaining about your hotel room

Scenario

You are in Spain on holiday with a group of friends. When you check into your hotel room, there is no running water in the bathroom. Your partner will play the part of the hotel manager, and you will complain.

Preparation

Follow the same procedure as you did for **Exercise 3**. Some facts that you might want to include in your conversation might be your name, your room number, what is wrong and what you would like him/her to do about it.

Role-play

Now you are ready to try out your role-play with a partner. Why not work with someone in your class, or see if your teacher or some other Spanish speaker would like to try out the role-play with you?

Finally try listening to the version of this role-play on the CD, then practise your role-play with the second version on the CD.

TRACK 58

TRACK 59

PAGES 53–54

Speaking tests – general conversation

The third and final Speaking test you will do is a general conversation. This could be about anything that you are studying in the course. This is probably the most difficult type of Speaking test to prepare for, but it is probably the easiest to do **if** you follow a few simple rules:

1. Prepare **well** for the conversation – your teacher will normally give you plenty of warning that you will be doing a test – by familiarising yourself with as much as possible of the material that you have studied for the topic.

2. Listen to as much Spanish as possible – all of the Spanish on the CD for this course will be helpful in general conversations.

3. Speak as much Spanish as possible in class with your teacher, friends or another Spanish speaker.

4. Practise the other Speaking exercises in this book as much as possible with other speakers and with the CD.

TRACK 60

Exercise 5 – General conversation about the world of work

Now try listening to the conversation on the CD where a girl is talking to her teacher about work experience and her plans for the future.

The second part of this conversation is recorded twice, once with both parts included and the second time with gaps for the parts said by the Scottish girl. In that part of the conversation the teacher's questions are general so that you can practise your own version of the conversation.

TRACK 61

PAGES 54–55

Transcripts

TRACK 46

Section 1 – Pronunciation Guide

The Spanish Alphabet

a; b; c; ch; d; e; f; g; h; i; j; k; l; ll; m; n; ñ; o; p; q; r; rr; s; t; u; v; w; x; y; z.

The three pronunciations of 'c'

casa; tocar

chocolate con churros

cielo; hacer

The pronunciation of 'z'

zorro; azul

The pronunciation of the 'jota' sound

jardín; ojalá

gerente; agente

The pronunciation of 'double l'

llamada; callar

The pronunciation of 'n tilde'

niño; año

TRACKS 47–52

Section 2 – Useful words and phrases

Refer to the vocabulary lists on pages 42 to 44.

Section 3

TRACK 53

Exercise 1 – Prepared talk: Personal information, version A

Me llamo Andrew. Tengo 15 años. Vivo en Dundee. En mi familia hay cuatro personas: mi madre, mi padre, mi hermana y yo. Mi madre se llama June y tiene 40 años. Ella es ama de casa. Mi padre se llama David y tiene 42 años. Él es fontanero. Mi hermana se llama Lyndsey y tiene 10 años. Ella está en la escuela primaria. En mi colegio hay 600 estudiantes y 40 profesores. Yo estudio ocho asignaturas. El inglés, las matemáticas, la historia, la química, la física, la música, la informática y el español. En mi tiempo libre me gusta escuchar música, jugar al fútbol e ir a las discotecas el fin de semana.

Section 4

Exercise 1 – Prepared talk: Personal information, version B

TRACK 54

Hola, me llamo Andrew. Tengo 15 años y vivo en una ciudad en el noreste de Escocia que se llama Dundee. Bueno ... Somos cuatro personas en mi familia: mi padre, mi madre, mi hermana y yo. Mi madre, que se llama June, tiene 40 años y es ama de casa. Mi padre, David, tiene 42 años y es fontanero. Me llevo bastante bien con mis padres, pero mi padre es muy estricto. Por eso, me llevo mejor con mi madre. Mi hermana pequeña se llama Lyndsey. Tiene sólo 10 años y está todavía en la escuela primaria. No me llevo bien con ella. Hay siempre disputas en casa, sobre todo cuando yo quiero ver el fútbol en la televisión y ella no. Voy a un colegio grande en el centro de la ciudad. En mi instituto hay más o menos 600 estudiantes y unos 40 profesores. Me gusta bastante el colegio porque tengo muchos amigos allí. Pero tengo mucho trabajo puesto que estudio ocho asignaturas. Las asignaturas que me gustan bastante son el inglés, la historia, la música y la informática. Las que no me gustan son las matemáticas, la química y la física. El español me da igual. Pues, con todo el trabajo que tengo que hacer por el colegio no tengo mucho tiempo libre. Cuando puedo, me gusta escuchar música y jugar al fútbol con mis compañeros. Pero lo que más me gusta es el fin de semana, cuando no hay colegio, salir a la discoteca con mi novia. Lo pasamos bomba.

Section 5

Exercise 2 – Prepared talk about your town

TRACK 55

Edimburgo es la capital de Escocia. Está situado en el sureste del país en el río Forth. Es una ciudad muy histórica con un castillo, el parlamento escocés y muchos monumentos – sobre todo en la zona que se llama The Royal Mile.

Bueno, en cuanto al clima, para los españoles a lo mejor no será muy bueno. Llueve bastante, pero no hace mucho frío y tampoco hay mucha nieve.

Hay mucho que hacer para los turistas en Edimburgo. Hay muchos grandes almacenes para los que aman ir de compras; para los aficionados del deporte hay muchos polideportivos, pistas de patinaje y una piscina muy famosa – The Commonwealth Pool; y para los aficionados de la cultura hay un montón de cines, bibliotecas, museos y teatros – destacan entre ellos The National Library of Scotland y The National Museum of Scotland, es decir la biblioteca y el museo nacionales.

Cada año en el verano, hay un festival internacional que atrae actores y artistas de todas partes del mundo – por no mencionar millares de turistas.

Section 6

Exercise 3 – Role-play – Arranging to go to a football match – Version A

Hola, Juan. ¿Qué tal estás?

Yo estoy bien, gracias. ¿Y tú?

Muy bien, gracias.

¿Te interesa el fútbol?

Sí, me interesa bastante. Yo soy aficionado del Barça. ¿Por qué me preguntas eso?

Bueno, es que mi equipo, el *Raith Rovers,* tiene un partido el miércoles por la tarde. ¿Qué te parece si vamos al fútbol?

Sí, estupendo. ¿A qué hora empieza el partido?

El partido empieza a las ocho menos cuarto.

Muy bien. Y el estadio, ¿queda lejos de tu casa?

No entiendo. ¿Quieres repetir la pregunta, por favor?

Nada más quería saber si tu casa está cerca del estadio o lejos del estadio.

Pues, sí. Mi casa está bastante cerca del estadio.

Perfecto. ¿Cómo podemos ir al estadio?

Bueno, en el coche de mi padre. Mi padre vendrá al hotel para buscarte sobre las siete. ¿Vale?

Vale. Hasta el miércoles, entonces.

Sí, hasta luego.

Section 7

Exercise 3 – Role-play – Arranging to go to a football match – Version B

....

Yo estoy bien, gracias. ¿Y tú?

....

Sí, me interesa bastante. Yo soy aficionado del Barça. ¿Por qué me preguntas eso?

....

Sí, estupendo. ¿A qué hora empieza el partido?

....

Muy bien. Y el estadio, ¿queda lejos de tu casa?

....

Nada más quería saber si tu casa está cerca del estadio o lejos del estadio.

....

Perfecto. ¿Cómo podemos ir al estadio?

....

Vale. Hasta el miércoles, entonces.

....

Section 8

Exercise 4 – Role-play – Complaining about your hotel room – Version A

TRACK 58

Perdone, señora,

Sí, ¿En qué puedo servirle?

Es que tengo un problema.

¿Sí?

Me llamo James Thompson y estoy aquí con el grupo escocés que acaba de llegar.

Bueno, ¿en qué consiste su problema?

Yo estoy en la habitación número 210 y en el cuarto de baño, no hay agua corriente.

O, lo siento mucho. ¿Le gustaría mudarse a otra habitación?

Lo siento, no entiendo. Quiere hablar más despacio, por favor.

Pues ... sí, discúlpeme. ¿Quiere otra habitación?

Sí, gracias, si es posible.

A ver ... Sí, hay otra habitación que está en la misma planta. El número 224. ¿Qué le parece?

Muy bien gracias. ¿Quiere repetir el número, por favor?

¿Cómo no? Se trata del 224, dos, dos, cuatro. A ver si hay alguien que le ayude con sus maletas.

Gracias.

TRACK 59

Section 9

Exercise 4 – Rôle-play – Complaining about your hotel room – Version B

....

Sí, ¿En qué puedo servirle?

....

¿Sí?

....

Bueno, ¿en qué consiste su problema?

....

O, lo siento mucho. ¿Le gustaría mudarse a otra habitación?

....

Pues ... sí, discúlpeme. ¿Quiere otra habitación?

....

A ver ... Sí, hay otra habitación que está en la misma planta. El número 224. ¿Qué le parece?

....

¿Cómo no? Se trata del 224, es decir dos, dos, cuatro. A ver si hay alguien que le ayude con sus maletas.

....

Section 10

Exercise 5 – General conversation about the world of work – Version A

Hola, Kerry, ¿qué hay?

Bastante bien, gracias.

No estuviste la semana pasada, ¿verdad?

Sí. Es que estaba trabajando.

Y ¿qué tal?

Bastante bien, gracias.

¿Dónde estuviste?

Estuve en la oficina de una agencia de publicidad en Glasgow.

¡Qué bien! ¿Cómo conseguiste ese trabajo?

Mi tío trabaja en la compañía, así que resultó fácil organizar la estancia allí.

¡Qué suerte! ¿Te gustó el trabajo?

Sí, me gustó bastante.

TRACK 60

¿Qué hiciste en la oficina?

Bueno, tuve que repartir el correo, sacar fotocopias, contestar el teléfono y confirmar citas con los clientes de la agencia.

¿Era interesante la experiencia?

No. Era bastante aburrido. Los colegas eran muy simpáticos y, al final de la semana me regalaron un CD ... pero, ya sé que no me gustaría trabajar en una oficina.

Y entonces, ¿qué te gustaría hacer?

Me gustaría seguir estudiando e ir a la universidad.

¿Por qué?

Porque es mucho más fácil.

Section 11

Exercise 5 – General conversation about the world of work – Version B

Hola, Kerry, ¿qué hay?

....

No estuviste la semana pasada, ¿verdad?

....

Y ¿qué tal?

....

¿Dónde estuviste?

....

¡Qué bien! ¿Cómo conseguiste ese trabajo?

....

¡Qué suerte! ¿Te gustó el trabajo?

....

¿Qué hiciste en la oficina?

....

¿Era interesante la experiencia?

....

Y entonces, ¿qué te gustaría hacer?

....

¿Por qué?

....

Section 3: Reading

Reading is a very important skill: it is worth one third of the total marks for Standard Grade Spanish. This skill is assessed by exams, which you will sit at the end of the course and, in this section, we will help you to prepare for these.

Pistas   Hints and Tips

- Don't run out of time. Make sure you **do lots of practice questions** before the exam so that you can **pace yourself accurately** on the day.

- Be careful with questions where there is a picture. It is there to point you in the right direction not to give you the answer.

- **Read the whole question** (even the bit in English at the top!). The title will give you a good idea of what the text is about and may even help with some of the answers.

- **Check how many marks each part of each question is worth.** This is a guide to how much you need to write (and how much time you should spend on it).

- Look to see if there are any words in the text with numbers beside them. These are called 'glossed items' and you will find their meaning under the passage. They are there to save you from looking for unusual or difficult words in your dictionary and the meaning given is the one you need. There is no catch – this is a free gift from your examiner!

- Remember that your dictionary is a tool to help you. **Do not look up every word you do not know** – many of them will not help you find the answers you need. Indeed, you should ideally only be using a dictionary two or three times per question at most.

- Set aside a few minutes every day to **learn vocabulary** throughout your Standard Grade course. It might seem boring at the time but if you do this you will not waste valuable time looking up words which you really should know.

- When you do need to use your dictionary remember that **the endings of words change in Spanish**; verbs because of the subject or the tense; nouns because they're singular or plural; adjectives because they must match the noun they describe. For this reason, the ending of the word you find may not be exactly the same as the one in the question. Differences at the beginning of words are something else altogether and mean that you're looking up the wrong thing! Be careful!

- Take care with **words starting with capital letters**. There is no point in trying to find names of people or places in the dictionary!

- **Keep your answers simple**. Most times the obvious answer is the one that is wanted.

- **Don't have <u>extra</u> guesses at answers**. If you have too many 'shots' at answering a question just because you're not sure which of them is the right one you may well lose marks. This is called the 'Extraneous Rule' and you need to be careful with it. At the same time, there is nothing wrong with having a guess at an answer – just don't overdo it on any one question!

- Finally, you must **read over your answers**. They should be written in English and they should make sense! If you do not understand what you have written or if it makes you laugh out loud, the chances are it's not correct!

Foundation Level Reading exam questions

At Foundation Level, all the questions are 'supported' – you do not have to search for the answer in the text but instead are helped towards it by grids, True/False questions, gap-filling exercises, etc. In order to achieve the best results in your exam you should therefore concentrate firstly on the wording of the questions and secondly on the text itself. You should also be aware of the following:

The Grid Rule

Basically this means that if you give more information than you are asked for it is bound to be wrong and you will lose one of the marks you have gained, e.g. you are asked to tick **three** things and you tick **four**.

True/False Questions

You will be asked to put a tick in a box beside either 'True' or 'False'. Be careful that you indicate **clearly** what you want your answer to be. If you change your mind you must cross out your first answer – don't try to write the second one on top of it!

Gap–filling

Usually the gap you are asked to fill will be of only one word. Don't try to write a whole sentence – it won't fit into the space! Make sure you read carefully the words before **and** after the gap. This will help you decide what is missing.

Remembering the above, try the following questions, based on actual exam questions from the past. Each one has its own clues to help you arrive at the answers.

1. Foundation Reading 1998, Question 5

In a shop window you see a poster.

Aprenda Idiomas

* *Cursos intensivos de inglés y francés*

* *Desde junio hasta setiembre*

* *Estancias en familia en Inglaterra y Francia*

* *Programas a partir de los 10 años*

Alianza Internacional
Lengua y Cultura
Teléfono 514 25 58

In the table below, tick (✔) TRUE or FALSE beside each statement.   (3)

	True	False
You can learn English and French.		
You will be staying in a hotel.		
You must be under 10 years old to take part.		

Minipistas · little hints!

Note the asterisks. These show different important points in the advertisement. There are **three** marks available and **four** points here. It's a good bet you will find all the answers you want in this part of the text.

- Line 1: Decide which are the key words. Once you find them you will have your answer.

- Line 2: Can you find the word 'hotel' anywhere?

- Line 3: The number 10 is in the text but don't assume that this makes the sentence true. Look carefully at what else might be false.

The next two questions are examples of the 'gap-filling' type of question.

2. Foundation Reading 2000, Question 8

You are reading a magazine and find this survey about teenagers and pocket money.

> ### Dinero de bolsillo
>
> - *cincuenta por ciento de jóvenes tienen un trabajo temporal.*
> - *sesenta y cinco por ciento de ellos dicen que reciben suficiente dinero.*
> - *ochenta por ciento compran revistas o caramelos con su dinero.*
>
>
> ptas

Complete the sentences below.

(a) .... per cent of youngsters have a job. (1)

(b) Sixty-five per cent say they receive .... money. (1)

(c) Eighty per cent buy .... or .... with their money. (2)

Minipistas · little hints!

- Remember to read the introduction to the question – this one is clearly about pocket money so the picture is not going to add anything to your understanding. Notice that there are **three** main points to the text and **three** questions – spot the link!

  (a) Here you are looking for a number near the start of the text. Can you find it?

  (b) This is a clear case of needing to know the word before the gap and the word after. Find the Spanish for 'receive' and 'money' in the text and your answer will be literally in between the two.

  (c) Here the important word is 'buy'. Once you have found it you are nearly there. One last thing – be careful with the word **'caramelos'**. Does it actually mean what it looks as if it does?

3. Foundation Reading 2001, Question 11

Here are the details of a competition.

Cocina con Betty Espaguetis
¡¡Y Gana una Muñeca!!

¿Te gustan los espaguetis? ¿Es uno de tus platos preferidos? Inventa una receta con espaguetis como ingrediente y gana una de las 100 muñecas 'Betty Espaguetis'.

Envía tu receta antes del día 21 de junio a:
  Betty Espaguetis
  Apartado de Correos 35.019
  28082 Madrid

Busca la lista de ganadores el lunes, 28 de junio en este periódico.

Complete the following sentences.

(a) Your recipe must contain .... (1)

(b) You can win a .... (1)

(c) You must send in your recipe before the .... (1)

(d) You will find the list of winners in the .... (1)

Minipistas little hints!

- Look at the beginning of the text. The proper name (Betty) should give you a clue as to the type of 'character' being described in the text.

  (a) It may seem a bit obvious but remember that recipes usually contain food! Find the Spanish word for 'recipe' and your answer will be close by.

  (b) Now is the time to use your common sense. Even if you have never heard of **'Betty Espaguetis'** you should be able to find the meaning of the word **'muñeca'** in the dictionary. Be careful! It can mean more than one thing.

  (c) The key word here has to be 'before'. Find it and you have your answer.

  (d) There are no trick questions here. Think simple and obvious – look for the Spanish word for 'in'.

Finally we have the type of question where you must match the answer or information you are given at the bottom of the text to the correct part of the text itself. Usually you will be asked for a letter, but occasionally you may be asked to give a number (e.g. a telephone number) or a person's name.

4. Foundation Reading 1997, Question 9

You go to a bookshop to look for presents. You see a number of new books on display.

In the space provided, write the letter of the book you should buy for each of the following people.

(4)

Your brother who likes Science Fiction.	
Your aunt who loves to cook.	
Your friend who is interested in history.	
Your grandmother who loves detective stories.	

Minipistas) little hints!

- There are two ways of doing this question. The first involves reading all the Spanish words in the text and finding the ones you want – this being the better of the two for learning new Spanish words. The second involves looking first at the questions and finding the key words. This way is much quicker if you are running out of time in an exam. Which will you try this time?

- When you look at the questions, remember that these are types of book. You will not get too far if you try to find the Spanish for 'Science Fiction' or 'history'.

General Level Reading exam questions

At General Level some of the questions are supported and others are not. (Check the introduction to Foundation Level for what 'supported' means.)

The following exercises are based on actual exam questions.

1. General Reading 1999, Question 4

You see this item in the newspaper.

> # Un delfín vivo permanece
> # siete horas en el Postiguet
>
> *Un delfín apareció ayer en la playa del Postiguet sobre las diez de la mañana.*
>
> *Muchas personas curiosas vinieron a ver al animal y los responsables en devolverlo al agua no lo retiraron de la arena hasta pasadas más de siete horas.*
>
> *La Policía Local se ocupó de trasladar al delfín hasta el parque Mundomar.*
>
> *Este tipo de incidente es poco corriente en esta parte de la costa.*

In the grid below, tick (✔) TRUE or FALSE beside each of the following statements. (3)

	True	False
The dolphin appeared yesterday.		
It was taken away at seven o'clock.		
Dolphins rarely appear in this area.		

Minipistas little hints!

- This time you are asked to tick True or False. Check the hints given for Foundation Level for this type of question.

- Which is the key word in the first sentence in English? Remember the answer to the first question is probably near the start of the text.

- Be careful with the time in the second part.

- The most important word here is 'rarely'. If you are not sure how to say this in Spanish use your dictionary.

SECTION 3

2. General Reading 1999, Question 2

You find an article about the footballer Luis Enrique.

Ficha Técnica

Nombre:	*Luis Enrique Martínez*
Nació:	*Gijón, Asturias, 8 de mayo de 1970*
Mide:	*1,80 m*
Pesa:	*73 kilos*

Empezó jugando en el Sporting en 1988. Vistió desde el 91 hasta el 96 la camiseta del Real Madrid. Lleva ya ocho años jugando con los colores del Barcelona.

Pasatiempos:	*Leer, el cine y el surf*
Gustos:	*La música, la ciudad de Gijón, el zumo de fruta, llevar ropa cómoda*

Fill in the gaps below to complete the sentences.

(a) Luis Enrique has played for Barcelona for .... years.   (1)

(b) His hobbies are ...., the cinema and surfing.   (1)

(c) His favourite drink is ....   (1)

(d) He likes wearing .... clothes.   (1)

Minipistas) little hints!

- Gap-filling exercises can cause a lot of problems but not if you use your common sense and think before answering.

- We know from the introduction who Luis Enrique is. Various teams are mentioned. You just have to find the information about the right one.

- Find the Spanish for 'hobbies' and you'll have your answer to question (b).

- You may not find the word for 'drink' so concentrate on the 'favourite' part.

- Be careful! Words can have more than one meaning. Be sure to choose the right one.

3. General Reading 1998, Question 8

You read this article about winning and losing teams.

Equipos Ganadores	**...Y Perdedores**
* *tienen metas claras*	* *no tienen grandes ambiciones*
* *ayudan a los miembros con problemas*	* *no aceptan diferentes puntos de vista*
* *celebran sus victorias*	* *les falta confianza*
* *evitan los conflictos internos*	* *no quieren admitir sus dificultades*
* *trabajan de forma coordinada*	* *no les importan los resultados*

(a) List **three** characteristics of a winning team. (3)

(b) List **three** characteristics of a losing team. (3)

Minipistas little hints!

- As you can see right away, this is not a 'supported' question but there is one aspect of the layout that is a clear pointer to where your answers will be. What is it?

- Be careful if you use your dictionary in this question. It is not enough to find a meaning and assume it is the correct one. Be aware of 'context'.

- Similarly you must not look up individual words and translate them. Your answers must make sense as **groups of words**, **phrases** or **sentences**.

4. General Reading 2000, Question 3

This leaflet is delivered to your friend's house.

Deportes para todos
¡Hay que visitarlo!
Gran apertura[(1)] **la próxima semana**
Los martes 10% descuento   * *piscina*
para los jóvenes   * *salón de belleza*
* *guardería*
abierto todos los días 08.00 hasta 22.00
[(1)]*apertura = opening*

(a) When will this new sports centre open for the first time? (1)

(b) What special offer is there for young people? (1)

(c) Name **three** facilities available at the centre. (3)

Minipistas little hints!

- Note the glossed word **'apertura'**. Could this be a clue as to where you'll find your first answer?

- Be careful to give as full an answer as possible, although there is only 1 mark for this.

- This question is asking for **three** separate answers. Can you see where those **three** answers might be found?

5. General Reading 2000, Question 9

This item in a magazine attracts your attention.

Elefantes Futbolistas

Tailandia es un país donde el elefante es más que el animal nacional. Normalmente se usa como medio de transporte o excavadora, pero una vez al año hay un original partido de fútbol donde los jugadores son elefantes.

No son tan ágiles como Rivaldo o Raúl, pero la pasión es comparable a la de todos los estadios de la liga española. La ventaja[1] principal que tienen los elefantes es que son muy grandes y fuertes. Además... tienen buena memoria.

[1]ventaja = advantage

(a) Give **one** way in which elephants are normally used in Thailand. (1)

(b) How often do these elephants play football? (1)

(c) What main advantage do they have as footballers? (1)

6. General Reading 2001, Question 10

You find this article about football.

El fútbol ¡No!

Los dueños de restaurantes y bares están tan enfadados con el fútbol, que piensan protestar a finales de octubre. Les gusta mucho este deporte, pero para ellos el problema es el horario de las transmisiones los sábados. Los partidos de fútbol terminan muy tarde y por eso los bares y los restaurantes están casi vacíos, perdiendo 660,000 euros cada temporada.

(a) What aspect of televised football do bar and restaurant owners **not** like?   (1)

(b) Explain how their business suffers.   (1)

Credit Level Reading exam questions

At Credit Level you can expect to be answering questions on fairly lengthy pieces of writing but don't let that put you off. The passages (usually four of them) will be laid out to make it possible for you to spot where the answers are without too much difficulty.

Pistas Hints and Tips

Remember:

- You may be given some 'supported' marks (up to a maximum of five) but this will not happen in every exam.

- You will probably be given some '**glossed**' words. Don't forget to look!

- The questions will be in order – the answer to the first one will be near the beginning of the text, the second will come next and the final answer will be nearest the end of the text.

- You are not expected to know every word in the passage and you do not need to. Use the questions as a guide to the parts of the text on which you should concentrate.

Now work your way through the following questions. Each one should take you 15 minutes at most.

1. Credit Reading 1998 Question 2

Later, you come across this article about the actor Antonio Banderas.

¿Qué es lo que más te gusta de tu profesión?

En primer lugar debo decirte que para mí ser actor es lo mejor de lo mejor. Tiene muchas ventajas. Por ejemplo, te permite realizar tus sueños, hacer amistades, llevar una vida diferente... Pero hay que reconocer que también tiene un lado negativo.

No puedes tener mucha vida privada, siempre estás viajando de un lado a otro. A pesar de todo es mi elección. Si algún día me canso o me aburro, cambiaré.

Dicen que los actors son una gente rara. ¿Es verdad?

Pues sí, somos bastante extraños. Constantemente tenemos que dar algo a los demás, hablar con la gente, ser abiertos. Pero también necesitamos atención, encerrarnos en el personaje, y eso nos provoca cierta inseguridad. Es una cosa psicológica.

¿Qué piensas hacer en el futuro?

Tengo un carácter creativo y abierto y siempre me ha gustado mucho hacer fotos y tocar el piano. Un día de estos me encantaría dirigir películas y abrir una escuela para jóvenes actores pero ¿sabes una cosa? De momento me encuentro muy contento con la vida que tengo.

(a) What does he see as the advantages of his profession? (2)

(b) What are its disadvantages? (2)

(c) What would he like to do in the future? (2)

Pistas Hints and Tips

- Remember that your answers must be based on the passage. Being Antonio Banderas' biggest fan does not guarantee any marks.

- The passage is divided into three and there are three questions. Is this helpful or not?

- Look for the Spanish for 'advantages'. You will see a number of things listed after it. Be careful! There are two marks available so don't write too much.

- What is the Spanish for 'disadvantages'? If the word from the dictionary is not there, think about how else this might be phrased.

- Don't confuse what he does with what he **would like** to do. You could make a note of how to say 'I like', 'I liked' and 'I would like'. These words will definitely be useful for all the parts of the examination.

2. Credit Reading 1998 Question 3

In the same magazine you read an article about the Jews saved by Oskar Schindler during the war.

Los Judíos de Schindler

Cuando la Guerra terminó, el hombre de negocios Oskar Schindler estaba completamente arruinado. Se había gastado toda su fortuna, cuatro millones de marcos alemanes, en proteger y salvar a mil trescientos judíos capturados por los Nazis. Para darle las gracias, los judíos supervivientes decidieron ayudar a Schindler. Todos los años le enviaban al negociante el dinero que habían ganado en un día de trabajo. Hasta el mismo día de su muerte en 1974, a los sesenta y seis años de edad, Schindler recibió una pensión de los judíos. Hoy su viuda sigue recibiendo esta pensión.

Muchos de los judíos han colaborado con Stephen Spielberg en su película Shindler's List, explicando cada detalle de los campos de concentración. También ayudaron al actor Liam Neeson ('Oskar Schindler') con su interpretación del personaje, al indicarle el comportamiento de Schindler, su forma de hablar y su manera de moverse. Además, en los últimos minutos de Schindler's List, rodada en Israel, algunos de ellos relataron sus experiencias delante de la cámara – narraciones que hicieron llorar no sólo a Spielberg sino también a todos los que han visto la película.

Los judíos de Schindler han tenido descendencia. Hoy en día son seis mil los que honran su nombre en todo el mundo.

Reading

(a) In what way did Schindler's Jews decide to help him? (3)

(b) In the making of the film *Schindler's List*, how did the Jews help the actor Liam Neeson? (3)

(c) What contribution did the Jews make at the end of the film? (2)

Minipistas little hints!

On the face of it this is a long and difficult passage. If you are not careful you can spend a lot of time trying to understand a lot of Spanish you don't need. In the exam you will be better served by concentrating on the questions. When you have completed the question in exam time, spend extra time using this passage to improve your vocabulary.

- In order to find the answer to the first question you need to find the words for 'Jews' and 'help'. Be very careful with the word '**ganado**'. The meaning you find first in the dictionary may not be the one you are looking for. Ask yourself if your answer makes sense.

- In the second question you are given a huge clue in the shape of Liam Neeson (or at least his name!) Remember – you are looking for **three** items.

- Think of another way of saying 'at the end of'.

3. Credit Reading 1999 Question 1

You read an interview with David Meca, a record-breaking swimmer.

El Tiburón Humano

David Meca admite que está loco. El pasado 16 de febrero batió el récord del Mundial de natación en aguas abiertas al nadar 88 kilómetros en ¡8 horas, 39 minutos y 25 segundos.

Es de Sabadell (Barcelona) y acaba de cumplir 25 años. Mide 1,79 y pesa 63 kilos.

¿Como es tu vida?

No muy normal. Me levanto muy temprano, a las 5 de la mañana. Durante el día hago dos entrenos de 10 a 15 kilómetros. Asisto a clases de Drama y suelo hacer dos horas de siesta. Casi no tengo tiempo libre pero el fin de semana me gusta salir.

¿Cuándo empezaste?

A los cinco años. Era bastante débil y el médico dijo que debía nadar.

¿Temes alguna cosa?

He nadado en el Pacífico, el Amazonas y el Nilo, en las mismas aguas que tiburones, cocodrilos y pirañas. Pero lo que más temo son las medusas.

¿Actor o nadador?

Ahora pesa más la natación. Y eso requiere dedicación absoluta. Dentro de unos años, será lo contrario.

(a) What is David Meca's opinion of himself? (1)

(b) Describe any **three** aspects of his daily routine. (3)

(c) He began swimming at the age of five. Why? (1)

(d) What does he fear most? (1)

Minipistas little hints!

This type of text (an interview) is one that is quite often used at Credit Level. The question/answer format should give you clear guidelines.

- Note that there is a difference between what he thinks of **himself** and what he says about **his life**. Don't confuse the two.

- You will find that there are more than three details to choose from. Be careful with the word **'asisto'**.

- Straightforward question = straightforward answer.

- Note particularly the word 'most'. Which Spanish word must you look for?

4. Credit Reading 2001 Question 1

You find this article about windsurfing.

Reglas del windsurfista

Hoy en día el windsurfing es uno de los deportes acuáticos más populares en España, especialmente en verano, pero hay que decir que también es un deporte que requiere cierto cuidado:

1. *Cuando sea posible, practica el windsurfing en zonas alejadas de los bañistas.*

2. *Infórmate de las características del lugar donde vas a navegar – por ejemplo vientos, corrientes, mareas[1]...*

3. *Siempre trata de informar a alguien de adónde vas y cuándo piensas volver.*

4. *Ten cuidado con los vientos de tierra y no te alejes mucho de la costa.*

5. *Si se te presentan problemas, nunca abandones la tabla porque es tu bote salvavidas.*

6. *No salgas al mar a última hora, al atardecer.*

[1]*mareas = tides*

(a) When possible, in what kind of area should you try to windsurf? (1)

(b) You are advised to tell someone that you are going out to sea. What information should you give them? (2)

(c) If you have problems while out surfing, what should you never do? Why not? (2)

(d) At what time of day should you not go surfing? (1)

Minipistas little hints!

In this type of question the layout is specifically designed to help you find the correct answers.

- Use the words of the question, especially the first phrase, to locate the answer.

- Be careful. The words '**Infórmate**' and '**informar**' are similar. Which one indicates the answer?

- The key here is the word 'never'. Take care with your English.

- You are given two expressions that amount to the same answer. Do not write two things that contradict each other. You only need one. Be careful with your English in this answer.

5. Credit Reading 1999 Question 3

You read this article in a magazine.

Hacer de 'au pair'

En países como Inglaterra, Canadá, Irlanda, Alemania, Italia, Estados Unidos y España existen agencias donde un equipo joven de chicas, y últimamente de chicos, experimentan la aventura de viajar haciendo de 'au pair'.

Las edades están comprendidas entre los 18 años mínimo y los 23-24 máximo y se requiere un conocimiento básico de la lengua del país, así como un tiempo de estancia mínimo de seis meses.

Cuando las chicas acuden a la agencia a hacer la solicitud, se les hace rellenar un tipo de cuestionario donde cuenta mucho la religión, los estudios realizados, la educación, el idioma, etcétera. Además, ellas también pueden pedir un tipo de condiciones, como por ejemplo que los niños tengan una edad determinada, número de hermanos, lugar de preferencia (mar, montaña...)

En España las 'au pair' tienen libre el domingo y el jueves por la tarde y tienen que trabajar seis horas diarias. A veces se les deja unas horas para que puedan acudir a clases e ir perfeccionando el idioma, objetivo principal por el que realizan este tipo de trabajo.

Natali Comets es una francesa de 21 años que lleva cinco meses viviendo en casa de una familia alicantina:

'Aquí mi deber – dice Natali – es cuidar de dos niñas de 4 a 7 años, hacer sus habitaciones, prepararles la comida, planchar su ropa y llevarles de paseo. La ventaja es que la familia tiene una señora que viene a limpiar la casa y por eso yo me dedico exclusivamente a las niñas.'

(a) Apart from age restrictions, what conditions are placed on anyone wanting to be an au pair? (2)

(b) Describe the average working week for an au pair in Spain. (2)

(c) What makes Natali's job easier? (1)

Minipistas   little hints!

Here we have a sample of the type of passage to be used at Credit Level to link with the world of work. Although it seems long it is not particularly difficult.

- Look for the first answer near the beginning of the text. You should be able to find the section on age quite easily. The other conditions should be listed close by.

- There are two marks available here – one for each complete piece of information. Be very careful with numbers.

- The use of the proper name 'Natali' makes this much more straightforward.

Answers to exam questions

Foundation Level Reading

1. True

   False

   False

2. (a) fifty

   (b) enough

   (c) magazines, sweets

3. spaghetti

   doll

   21 June

   newspaper

4. E

   A

   F

   C

General Level Reading

1. True

   False

   True

2. (a) eight

   (b) reading

   (c) fruit juice

   (d) comfortable

3. (a) 3 from:

   they have clear goals/aims

   they help members of the team who have problems

   they celebrate their victories

   they avoid internal conflict

   they work in a co-ordinated manner

   (b) 3 from:

   they do not have great ambitions

   they do not accept different points of view

   they lack confidence

   they do not want to admit to their difficulties

   they do not care about results

4. (a) next week

   (b) 10% discount on Tuesdays

   (c) swimming pool

   beauty salon

   crèche

5. (a) 1 from:

   as a means of transport

   as a digger

   (b) once a year

   (c) they are big and strong

6. (a) the times the matches are on TV

    (b) The bars and restaurants are almost empty/they lose 660,000 euros

Credit Level Reading

1. (a) 2 from:

    you can fulfil your dreams

    you can make friends

    you can lead a different life

    (b) you do not have much of a private life

    you are always travelling from one place to another

    (c) direct films

    open a school for young actors

2. (a) every year

    they sent him the money

    they earned in one day

    (b) they told him how Schindler behaved

    how he spoke

    how he moved

    (c) they recounted their experiences

    in front of the cameras

3. (a) he thinks he's mad

    (b) 3 from:

    gets up early/at five a.m.

    does two training sessions of 10 to 15 kilometres

    attends a Drama class

    usually has a two hour nap

    (c) 1 from:

    he was quite weak

    doctor said he should start

    (d) jellyfish

4. (a) far from bathers

    (b) where you are going

    when you intend to return

    (c) abandon your surfboard

    it is your lifeboat

    (d) at nightfall/dusk

5. (a) basic knowledge of the language of the country

    minimum stay of six months

    (b) free on Sunday and Thursday afternoon/evening

    have to work six hours a day

    (c) family employs woman who comes to clean the house

More reading practice using original reading material

This section contains some new passages for you to use as reading practice. You will find that they become more and more difficult (with an easy one here and there to keep you going!) so try to get a little further each time you work with these passages. There are some hints to help you along but not as many as for the questions based on the past papers, so you'll have practice working more independently.

Question number one

You are given this leaflet about a special offer from a pizza company.

Minipistas

There are only a few words you need to know in order to be able to do this question.

Which ones are they? Look at the English first!

Telepizza

Mediana Gratis

Gratis – una pizza mediana al comprar una pizza familiar

- *cuatro o más ingredientes,*
- *de igual o menor valor la segunda*
- *válida los siete días de la semana*

In the grid below tick (✔) TRUE or FALSE beside each statement. (3)

	True	False
You get a medium pizza free with a family sized one.		
You can only have four ingredients.		
The offer is not valid at weekends.		

Question number two

You pick up a card in the bank.

Minipistas

Use the bullet points! You have been given the meaning of the first one, so work on the other two for your answers.

Hagamos algo juntos

- *por la cultura*
- *por el medio ambiente*
- *por nuestro futuro*

CAM   *Caja de Ahorros del Mediterráneo*

Complete the sentence below.

We should be working together for culture, for ....

and for .... (2)

Question number three

You are handed a piece of paper in the street.

> # Invitación
>
> *Vale por Dos Raciones de Pollo Asado*
>
> *Los organizadores de la fiesta en honor a Santa Bárbara quieren agradecer simbólicamente con una invitación de pollo asado a los asistentes a la fiesta que tendrá lugar en la Alameda de Valencia el día 2 de marzo. Este cupón podrá ser canjeado por dos raciones de pollo asado (hasta agotar existencias) y al presentarlo tendrá un tratamiento preferencial en el reparto.*

Complete the sentence below.

This coupon entitles you to .... (2)

Minipistas — little hints!

- If you visit a busy Spanish resort during the summer you will be used to seeing people giving out leaflets about discos, cafes, bars, etc. These may contain loads of Spanish you have not seen before but usually the information you need is summed up in two or three words. The two or three words you need in this case are actually repeated three times. What are they?

- Notice that there are two marks for this question. Why do you think this is?

Question number four

Here is a leaflet about the facilities offered on a particular rail journey.

Prestaciones a bordo y servicios complementarios

Acompañamiento de menores

Cuatro canales de música

Aseo para bebés

Espacios para equipajes voluminosos

Acceso a Salas Club

Prensa diaria y revistas

Copa de bienvenida a bordo

Aparcamiento (incluido en el precio del billete)

In the grid below put a tick beside the **four** services on offer.

toilets for babies	
reclining seats	
space for bulky luggage	
air-conditioning	
films	
newspapers and magazines	
restaurant	
free parking	

Minipistas little hints!

- It's a good idea to have a very quick look at the question to see first if there are any really obvious answers.

- After doing the easy stuff, try to focus on the individual words in the question that you think will give you the answers. For example, what is the Spanish for 'seats'? (Incidentally, it's usually easier to look for nouns rather than verbs or adjectives in the dictionary, so try to find 'seats' rather than 'reclining'.)

Question number five

You read this little article in a magazine

Entender al hámster

El hámster es fácilmente adaptable a la vida doméstica. Sólo hay que respetar su horario y no molestarle, puesto que se trata de un animal nocturno. Así que no debes despertarle porque podría morderte, aunque no es habitual. Hay que acostumbrarle a nuestra presencia cogiéndole e incluso dándole de comer en la mano. Si algo no le gusta se pone de pie y rechina los dientes.

Complete the sentences below.

(a) You should not disturb a hamster because he is a .... (1)

(b) If you waken him, he may .... (1)

(c) If he does not like something, he ....

    and .... (2)

Minipistas little hints!

- Check the Spanish for 'disturb' – the answer will not be far away.

- Once again, find the Spanish for a particular word – 'to waken'.

- What's the Spanish for 'to like'? Two phrases follow it. Find out what they mean and you're done!

Question number six

In a television magazine you see the following short article about a new programme.

La Quinta Esfera

De lunes a viernes a las 19:30 horas se emite el nuevo concurso de Telecinco. Jorge Fernández es el encargado de presentarlo y dirigir a los seis concursantes que se enfrentan cada día por un premio en metálico que está comprendido entre 150·000 y 300·000 euros.

Los participantes tienen que demostrar su habilidad a lo largo de cinco rondas eliminatorias respondiendo a preguntas de todos los ámbitos.

Sólo durante la primera semana del casting se han recibido 4·000 llamadas para participar.

Minipista

Find the numbers in the passage and see what information is given round each one.

Complete the grid with the correct numbers. (4)

the number of competitors every day	
the maximum number of euros they can win	
the number of rounds in a programme	
the number of people wanting to take part in the first week	

Question number seven

You read a leaflet about a nature park in Madrid.

Siente el frío helado de los polos

Vive las tormentas tropicales

Ve nacer a una mariposa

Descubre las criaturas que se mueven cuando cae la noche

Observa cómo se organiza una colmena por dentro

Experimenta el nacimiento de las aves en el nido

Las aventuras más emocionantes se viven en

Faunia

el parque temático de la naturaleza en Madrid.

There are many things that you can do in this park. What are some of them? Complete the sentences below.

(a) You can feel .... (1)

(b) You can see .... (1)

(c) You can observe .... (1)

(d) You can experience .... (1)

Minipistas little hints!

- This question is a bit more difficult than the ones you have tackled so far in this section, but is still straightforward if you know what to look for.

- The main clue lies in the key words used in each of the sentences – feel, see, observe and experience. Use them to help locate your answers.

- Be careful with the word 'polos'. You may know it from a different context to this one.

- Think carefully before dashing to use your dictionary. You probably know more of these words than you might at first think. It's important not to waste time although there are words you'll need to look up.

Question number eight

You pick up a leaflet in a fastfood restaurant.

> ### Consejos de McDonald's
>
> *Para mejorar la dieta desde la infancia es conveniente recordar estos consejos:*
>
> - *Comer de todo, variada y moderadamente*
> - *Organizar la alimentación en 3-4 comidas diarias y seguir un horario regular de comidas.*
> - *Dar mayor importancia al desayuno*
> - *Practicar deporte*
> - *Para conseguir un buen aporte de hierro, es importante incluir en la alimentación carnes y pescados.*

What advice is given about:

(a) the range of food you should eat? .... (3)

(b) the timing of meals? .... (2)

(c) breakfast? .... (1)

(d) iron? .... (2)

Minipistas

Look carefully at the number of marks being given here and make sure you give all the necessary information. (This applies to all the questions here.)

What is the Spanish word for 'iron'? If you look it up make sure you choose correctly.

Question number nine

You see the following advertisement in a newspaper. It is about poverty in Peru.

> ## Se necesitan padrinos
>
> *En Perú miles de niños viven en situación de extrema pobreza*
>
> - *Deseo apadrinar*
> - *Deseo ayudar sin ser padrino*
> - *Deseo recibir información*
>
> *¡Ayúdanos a ayudar!*
>
>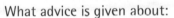
>
> *Coprodeli*
> *Paseo de la Habana 190, Bajo*
> *28036 Madrid*

The organisers of this campaign have given people 3 choices as to how they might take part. Explain what they are.

(3)

Minipistas little hints!

- You are asked for three choices and there are three sentences, each with a box beside it.

- Each of the sentences starts with the same word, so make sure you get it right. If necessary, look it up in the dictionary, but be careful! What kind of word is it?

- The word 'apadrinar' is obviously very important here. Make sure you find its correct meaning!

Minipistas

This is really quite an uncomplicated question. For each section, you need to focus on one obvious clue – the words for 'adventures', 'forget' and 'promise'. Remember that these will be either nouns or verbs and in your dictionary may not look exactly the same as they do in the text.

Question number ten

You read a leaflet about a special promotion organised by Telepizza and Terra Mitica, a huge theme park near Benidorm.

Terra Mítica y Telepizza

Disfruta de lo más guay

Con el pasaporte de nuestro club te convertirás en un auténtico aventurero.

Podrás convertirte en un auténtico gladiador, viajar por los Mares del Sur y buscar maravillosos tesoros ocultos.

Cada dos meses viviremos una aventura distinta.

Apúntate, consigue tu pasaporte y no te olvides de pegar las pegatinas.

Te prometemos que recibirás premios seguros y participarás en increíbles sorteos.

(a) The leaflet mentions three types of adventure you can take part in. What are they? (3)

(b) Once you have your passport, what must you not forget to do? (1)

(c) What two promises are made to you? (2)

Question number eleven

You are reading a leaflet about train travel.

Información de interés

Cuando adquiera su billete compruebe que los datos referentes a su viaje (fecha de viaje, hora de salida, etc.) se ajustan a su petición.

El control de acceso al tren permanence abierto hasta 2 minutos antes de su salida.

Por cada billete puede transportar una maleta y un bolso de mano o maletín (hasta 20 kilos).

En las estaciones de Barcelona, Valencia y Alicante, con billetes de clase Preferente: Acceso a Salas Club

Aparcamiento incluido en el precio del billete (24 horas viaje de ida, 48 horas viaje de ida y vuelta)

(a) According to the article, what should you check when you receive your ticket?

Give two examples (4)

(b) What are the rules regarding the luggage allowed per passenger? (3)

(c) What conditions are attached to the free parking entitlement? (3)

Minipistas

Not too many hints here! Just remember that the answers to the questions will be roughly at the beginning, in the middle and at the end of the text. One more thing – when you are looking for the Spanish word for 'check' remember that the form that you find in the dictionary may well not be identical to the one in the passage.

Question number twelve

On the letters page of a teenage magazine, *El Desván*, you see the following instructions.

Cinco ideas para escribir a 'El Desván'

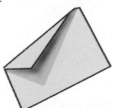

Si escribes a 'El Desván' lee atentamente estas instrucciones y nos ayudarás a agilizar la publicación de tu carta.

1. *Envía tu correspondencia al apartado de Correos 35.018, 28080 Madrid*

2. *Ahorra espacio. No escribas más de diez líneas.*

3. *No escribas demasiado. Expón claramente tus ideas.*

4. *En la parte de atrás del sobre no pongas tu dirección. Preferimos que hagas un buen dibujo. Cuanto mejor sea, más posibilidades tendrás de que tu carta salga publicada.*

5. *Escribe tu nombre y dirección solamente en el interior de la carta.*

Minipista

Take careful note of how many marks there are per question and watch out for the little word 'no'!

(a) What advice are you given about the length of your letter? (2)

(b) What is then said about **the way** in which you write? (2)

(c) What are you advised to put on the back of your envelope? Why? (3)

(d) Where should you write your name and address? (1)

Question number thirteen

You see a job advert in a local newspaper.

Minipista

Straightforward – look out for the key words in the statements in the grid and take it from there.

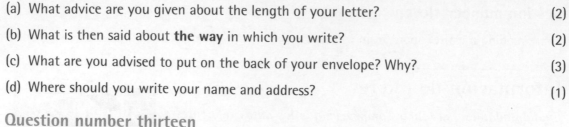

> ## Empresa Distribuidora de Gran Prestigio
>
> *solicita*
>
> *Vendedores de relojería*
>
> *Hombre o mujer con gran capacidad de relaciones públicas y edad máxima de 40 años.*
>
> *Imprescindible buena presencia*
>
> *Disponibilidad absoluta para viajar con vehículo propio.*
>
> *Se valorará experiencia.*
>
> *Ingresos muy interesantes*
>
> *Enviar currículum con foto reciente al apartado de correos 8081, 28008 Madrid*

In the grid below tick (✔) TRUE or FALSE beside each statement. (4)

	True	False
The job involves buying watches.		
You must be no more than 40.		
You will be given a company car.		
Experience does not matter.		

Question number fourteen

You read a little article about the most famous Spanish actress, Penélope Cruz.

> *Sus padres la tuvieron cuando sólo contaban con veinte años de edad y le pusieron el nombre de Penélope por una canción de Joan Manuel Serrat. Su padre se dedica al comercio y su madre es peluquera. Su hermana es bailarina de la compañía de Joaquín Cortés y su hermano va para futbolista.*
>
> *Penélope estudió nueve años de ballet clásico, tres años de baile español y un curso de danza jazz.*
>
> *Su carrera artística se inició en la televisión. También hizo spots publicitarios y un videoclip con el grupo musical Mecano.*
>
> *Sus amigos la llaman Pe, le gusta llevar ropa cómoda y escuchar la música clásica, no fuma ni bebe alcohol, le encanta la comida japonesa y los animales (tiene una gata llamada Aitana).*

Complete the sentences below.

(a) When Penelope was born her parents were .... (1)

(b) Her name comes from .... (1)

(c) Her brother is going to be .... (1)

(d) Penelope likes to wear .... (1)

(e) She loves ....

    and .... (2)

Question number fifteen

You read an announcement in the newspaper about some road repairs.

Disculpen las molestias

En la A-7, estamos realizando obras de mantenimiento del firme de la autopista.

Los próximos días 14 y 15 de julio, un carril de la Autopista permanecerá cortado unos 500 m dirección Valencia, desde las 22h hasta las 8h del día siguiente.

Hacemos lo posible para que estos inconvenientes sean los mínimos, trabajando día y noche, siempre que las condiciones atmosféricas lo permitan. Rogamos respeten la señalización especial establecida con motivo de las obras y circulen con precaución.

Muchas gracias por su colaboración.

(a) How is the company in charge trying to reduce the inconvenience suffered by motorists?   (1)

(b) What might make this difficult?   (1)

(c) What are motorists asked to do? Mention **two** things   (2)

Minipistas little hints!

- Although normally you will find the answer to the first question near the beginning this is not a hard and fast rule. Check for a word in the text which is close to 'inconvenience'.

- There is only one mark for part (b), so don't look for a long complicated answer.

- If you are asked to mention two things, do it. Do not give more than you are asked for or you will almost certainly give back one of the marks you have gained.

- Be careful with the word '**circulen**'.

Minipistas

Concentrate on the parts of the article which are relevant to the questions.

Make sure your answers (especially a and d) make sense!

Question number sixteen

In a magazine you come across an interesting article about the Tour de France cycle race.

El Tour cumple 100 años

¿Sabías que...?

El Tour surgió, como casi todas las pruebas deportivas importantes, de la propuesta de un periódico, L'Auto, y su creador fue el director de esta publicación, Henri Desgranges, que se encargaría de la dirección de las primeras carreras.

El primer maillot[(1)] amarillo lo vistió Eugene Christophe en 1919. Por cierto, no ganó la carrera de ese año, ya que se impuso el belga Lambot.

Sólo cuatro ciclistas han logrado vestir el jersey amarillo desde la primera hasta la última etapa: el italiano Bottecchia (1924), el luxemburgués Frantz (1928), el belga Romain (1935) y el francés Anquetil (1961).

Sólo cuatro españoles han ganado la ronda francesa: Bahamontes en 1959, Delgado en 1988 e Induráin en 1991, 1992, 1993, 1994 y 1995.

El francés Raymond Poulidor estuvo entre los tres primeros en ocho ocasiones, lo que constituye el record de podios. Curiosamente, nunca ganó el Tour.

La mayor distancia entre el ganador y el segundo clasificado se produjo en la primera edición, cuando el francés Garin le sacó en la general 2 horas, 49 minutos y 45 segundos a su compatriota Pathier. Y la menor ventaja es muy reciente, de 1989, cuando el estadounidense Lemond ganó con sólo 8 segundos de ventaja sobre el galo Fignon.

[(1)]*maillot = jersey*

Who were the following men?

(a) He created the Tour.   (1)

(b) He was the first to wear the yellow jersey.   (1)

(c) He was the last man to wear the yellow jersey from the start of the Tour to the finish.   (1)

(d) He holds the record for the number of appearances on the podium.   (1)

(e) He won the Tour by the smallest margin.   (1)

Minipistas little hints!

- Once again, we have a question which contains a lot of Spanish but which can be broken up into manageable chunks. Remember that the answers will be found in the order of the questions, i.e. the answer to part (a) will appear before the answer to part (b) and so on.

- You should be able to find the word for 'yellow' without any trouble. All you have to do is find it twice!

- Find the word for 'podium'. It's not as difficult as you might think!

Question number seventeen

You read this article in a local newspaper.

> *El más viejo y distante planeta jamás descubierto fue detectado por los astrónomos a unos 5.600 millones de años luz de la Tierra y constituye una amplia esfera gaseosa de unos 13.000 millones de años de antigüedad, informó ayer un grupo de astrónomos.*
>
> *Este descubrimiento podría cambiar las teorías acerca de cuándo ocurrió la formación de los planetas o cuándo la vida pudo haber evolucionado, dijeron los astrónomos en una rueda de prensa en la NASA. El planeta, que tiene más de dos veces el tamaño de Júpiter, orbita alrededor de dos estrellas que están vinculadas desde hace unos 1·000 millones de años.*
>
> *Ese sistema se encuentra en la constelación Escorpio dentro de un rácimo globular llamado M4 y que contiene estrellas que se formaron hace varios millones de años antes que el Sol y sus planetas.*

(a) In what two ways is this planet unique? (2)

(b) What influence might this discovery have? (3)

(c) The planet's system is in the constellation Scorpio. What is said about the stars within it? (2)

Question number eighteen

You read an interview with a young man who wishes to be a bullfighter.

Entrevista con un torero

Oscar Pérez quiere ser torero. Oscar tiene 16 años. Cada mañana entrena en la plaza de toros de Ecija (Sevilla). Por la tarde va a la escuela: 'Yo quiero ser un torero con cultura'. Oscar es muy buen estudiante: 'Me gustan las matemáticas, pero la historia no mucho.'

Entrena desde hace cuatro años. Oscar quiere ser un torero profesional. En agosto de 2002 Oscar debutó en la plaza de toros de su pueblo y mató un toro joven. '¿Por qué quiero ser torero? Porque es mi vocación. Toda mi vida, desde pequeño, he ido a la plaza de toros. Mi familia ama las corridas, aunque yo soy el único torero en la familia.'

Oscar tiene dos hermanos y tres hermanas. Su padre siempre va con él a la plaza de toros. Mientras, su madre está en casa y reza. '¿Miedo? Antes de salir estoy nervioso. Pero cuando estoy delante del toro no tengo miedo. Cuando estoy en la plaza mi mejor amigo es el toro. Es una gran sensación.'

También juega al tenis y visita a sus amigos. 'Pero un torero no va a la discoteca, ni bebe, ni fuma. La preparación física y la concentración son muy importantes.'

Minipistas

Although the subject matter of this passage is not difficult, the questions are a lot more open-ended than others you have seen. Part (b), in particular, will require you to read very carefully the second paragraph. Note that there are three marks for this section. What are these marks for? Be careful!

Minipistas

You should be able to find the answers you need without much difficulty.

You could use this passage as a source of some useful vocabulary. Read it a few times and make a note of all the words you don't know as well as making sure that you really do know all the ones you should! (e.g. school stuff, families, etc.)

(a) Describe a typical day for Oscar. (2)

(b) Why does he say he wants to be a bullfighter? (1)

(c) What do his parents do while he is fighting? (2)

(d) What does Oscar say is important for a bullfighter? (2)

Question number nineteen

Once again you have found an article about the TV programme 'La Quinta Esfera'. This one is a good bit harder than the one we've already seen (on page 79).

'La Quinta Esfera' ofrece tensión y preguntas inteligentes, pero además cuenta con el elemento diferenciador de que Jorge Fernández será la antítesis de lo que viene siendo habitual en este tipo de formatos en los que los participantes son sometidos a una enorme presión psicológica.

En el nuevo concurso de Telecinco, Jorge Fernández va más allá de ser un mero conductor de concurso para introducir el humor y la ironía sobre los diferentes aspectos personales de los competidores, comentando anécdotas y detalles de cada uno de ellos, con la finalidad de favorecer el clima y la puesta en escena a favor de los concursantes para calmar los nervios.

Además, los concursantes no sólo deben enfrentarse a diferentes mecánicas de juego en cada ronda sino que el tiempo es un elemento en su contra ya que tienen pocos segundos para responder a las diferentes preguntas.

(a) How does the presenter of this programme differ from those of other shows? (3)

(b) What is he trying to do for the competitors? (1)

(c) Which particular aspects of the competition make it difficult for those taking part? (2)

Minipistas little hints!

- Be careful with question (a). It asks you '**how**' something is done. It is not enough to repeat that the presenter is different from others.

- In question (b), note that there is only one mark for the answer, which means it is very straightforward. Do not write too much here.

- The word 'difficult' does not actually appear in the text. You need to look for something else – could the word for 'competitors' be helpful?

Question number twenty

Here is another of the popular interview type of question. This time it is about a young Spanish tennis-player.

Entrevista con Carlos Cuadrado, ganador del Roland Garros junior 2001

¿Estás satisfecho con la organización del campeonato y las instalaciones del club?

La verdad es que las pistas son muy buenas y los organizadores están trabajando mucho para que todo sea perfecto. Lo cierto es que todos estamos muy contentos y satisfechos con el club y las instalaciones.

¿Qué te ha parecido el nivel que has encontrado en el torneo? ¿Cuál es el ambiente entre los jugadores?

Hay muy buen ambiente, todos se están esforzando mucho. La verdad es que estamos jugando con un gran nivel y muy bien. Pero hace un calor terrible y el que gane va a tener que sudar lo suyo.

¿Qué aspiraciones tienes para este año como profesional?

Como tenista aspiro a ganar, si puedo. Pero si no lo consigo, sólo quiero jugar lo mejor posible y dar todo de mí en la pista. A nivel general, deseo participar en el mayor número de torneos que pueda este año. Bueno, todos los que mi cuerpo aguante. El próximo, de hecho, lo tengo en Elche.

(a) What two positive comments does he make about the tournament he is playing in?   (2)

(b) What particular problem are the players having to deal with?   (1)

(c) Generally speaking, what is Carlos' aim for this year?   (1)

Minipistas little hints!

- Both you and Carlos are asked three questions so it's a fair bet that each one of Carlos' answers will provide you with one of yours.

- Note that question (c) starts with the phrase 'generally speaking'. Very often, it's the first word or words in a question which provide you with the biggest clues about the whereabouts of the answers.

Question number twenty-one

Here is a passage relating to a very famous sportsman but you should not assume you know the answers simply because you may be one of his fans!

Tiger Woods está considerado el mejor golfista de todos los tiempos, con permiso del gran Jack Nicklaus. Se ha convertido en uno de esos deportistas llamados a ser inmortales.

Nació el 30 de diciembre de 1975 Eldrick, hijo de Earl Woods, un teniente de la Armada de los Estados Unidos, y Kultida, una nativa de Tailandia. Desde muy pequeño el niño fue conocido con el apodo de 'El Tigre' que su padre le puso en honor a su amigo Vuong Dang Phong, un soldado vietnamita.

El pequeño Eldrick parecía predestinado a ser una gran estrella del golf, como refleja una anécdota de cuando contaba seis meses de edad: empezó a imitar el swing de su padre, que estaba lanzando algunas bolas contra una red. A partir de entonces, Earl Woods comenzó a diseñar la carrera de su hijo para intentar convertirlo en una máquina de ganar dinero, a imagen y semejanza de lo que hizo Richard Williams, padre de las tenistas Venus y Serena.

Williams se quedó sorprendido un buen día al ver en la televisión a una tenista recibiendo un cheque con muchos ceros por haber ganado un torneo, así que decidió que sus dos hijas pequeñas harían lo mismo en un futuro. Y lo consiguió. El padre de Tiger Woods pensó lo mismo, aunque quizá no era consciente de que su hijo se convertiría en un mito. 'Lo eduqué para que fuera un gran campeón, pero lo que hice fue simplemente mostrarle el camino; el resto corrió por cuenta de él. El dinero fue algo que vino con el triunfo, pero él entendió muy bien que lo suyo era jugar bien para él y para la gente,' explica Earl.

En siete temporadas de profesional ha ganado 42 torneos, entre ellos siete del Grand Slam. Sus admiradores se cuentan por millones e incluyen a mitos del deporte, como Michael Jordan. 'Tiger Woods es mi único héroe en la Tierra. Lo veo jugar y todo lo hace con una extraña facilidad. ¡Lo suyo es talento puro!'

Sus más acérrimos fans incluso han creado los 10 mandamientos de 'El Tigre' y han construido en Internet la primera 'iglesia' de Woods. El único requisito para formar parte de este grupo de admiradores es sentir devoción por el número uno mundial y mencionar sus 'milagros' en los campos de golf.

(a) According to the article, from where did Tiger get his nickname? (1)

(b) When and how did he first show a talent for golf? (3)

(c) In what way is Earl Woods like Richard Williams? (1)

(d) How does Earl Woods sum up his part in Tiger's development? (2)

(e) How does Michael Jordan feel about Tiger? (1)

(f) What two developments show how fanatical some of Tiger's supporters have become? (2)

A much longer passage here, but the level of language used is not too difficult.

- The Spanish for 'nickname' is **'apodo'**.

- Note the three marks available for (b). You need to give a full answer to get them all.

- Question (d): This hint is probably too basic for you, but look for the part of the passage in which Earl Woods is quoted!

- The important word to answer (e) is 'feel'.

- Look towards the end of the passage to find the answer to (f). The vocabulary is straightforward with the possible exception of **'mandamientos'**. Use your dictionary to find its meaning.

Question number twenty-two

This next question is similar to the last one in that it refers to a very familiar personality.

Matt Groening

Nació el 15 de febrero de 1954 en Portland, Oregón. Comenzó su carrera como dibujante a muy temprana edad, de hecho desde primer día de clase. El mismo Groening manifestaba que cuanto más se enfadaba la maestra, de mayor calidad eran los dibujos que hacía.

En 1977 se graduó en la Escuela Estatal de Evergreen, en Olympia, Washington. Mientras que estuvo en Evergreen, Groening pasó la mayor parte de su tiempo trabajando en el periódico de la escuela. Más tarde se marchó a Los Angeles a comenzar su carrera de escritor, que es lo que de verdad quería ser.

La carrera de Matt Groening cambió radicalmente cuando creó un cínico cómic llamado 'La Vida en el Infierno' que se centraba en un conejo dibujado a trazos muy simples llamado Binky. Otros personajes eran Shcba, la novia de Binky; y dos personajes idénticos llamados Akbar y Jeff.

El 8 de septiembre de 1986 los Simpson hicieron su debut como un 'sketch' de 2 minutos en el Show de Tracey Ullman. Groening rápidamente dibujó cinco nuevos personajes para la presentación (los hizo en quince minutos).

Los Simpson se ganaron la inmediata aclamación de la crítica y de los seguidores cuando en 1990 debutaron como el programa de mayor audiencia de la Fox. Durante los siguientes 8 años la serie ha ganado un premio Emmy (los 'oscars' de la televisión) y ha hecho historia por convertirse en la serie de animación de mayor duración.

Minipistas

This passage is longer than those you will find in the final examination but will give you good practice in finding answers. In fact, you probably don't really need much help with this one. All the vocabulary is straightforward so just read carefully!

(continued...)

Aunque la familia Simpson no está basada en la familia de Matt Groening, sus nombres sí lo están: el padre y el hijo de Matt se llaman Homer. Su madre se llama Margaret y los nombres de sus hermanas pequeñas son Lisa y Maggie. Bart, por otro lado, es la modificación de la palabra 'brat' que en inglés significa 'mocoso'. Groening insiste en que Bart no es un retrato de sí mismo. Otros personajes, como el jefe Wiggum, están inspirados en nombres de algunas calles donde Groening creció.

Los Simpson se ha convertido en la más popular serie de animación del mundo. Mientras que los principales personajes han permanecido, la serie ha aumentado su reparto, incluyendo más personajes interesantes y cómicos. Pero lo que no ha cambiado es la habilidad de la serie para hacer al público pensar y reír cada día de emisión.

(a) When exactly did Matt Groening begin his career as an artist? (1)

(b) What was the immediate effect of this? (1)

(c) What was his real ambition in life? (1)

(d) How long did it take him to draw The Simpson family? (1)

(e) How has the series made history? (1)

(f) Where did the main characters get their names? (4)

(g) There have been many changes to the programme but in what way has it not changed? (1)

Question number twenty-three

Bullfighting, while still very popular in Spain, is also one of the fiercest sources of debate. Here is an article in which two young people give their views.

El debate

Carlos Gilbert tiene 15 años. Vive en Barcelona. Desde los tres años va a las corridas de toros con su familia. María Novellas tiene 17 años y también es de Barcelona. A María no le gustan las corridas de toros.

¿Piensas que las corridas son crueles y violentas? ¿Son el espectáculo de la muerte?

Carlos: Es cruel o violento porque hay sangre. Pero el aficionado no mira la sangre. El aficionado admira el arte y el poder del torero. También es cruel comer ostras, o la caza del zorro. El toro bravo es un toro para pelear. Los toros bravos existen para las corridas de toros.

María: Pienso que es violento y cruel. No me gusta ver las corridas de toros. No me gusta ver sufrir y morir un animal. Los toros bravos pueden existir sin las plazas de toros.

Las corridas de toros ¿son cultura? ¿son arte?

Carlos: Las corridas de toros son cultura porque se transmiten de generación en generación durante siglos. Están en la literatura, en la pintura, y muchos intelectuales son aficionados.

María: ¿Cultura? Pienso que cultura es otra cosa. No veo nada interesante en los toros. Para mí no son cultura.

¿La lucha toro-hombre es igual?

Carlos: Sí, porque se igualan las fuerzas del toro con las del hombre y entonces se enfrentan solos en la plaza.

María: No, porque hay un toro y varios hombres. El toro al final siempre muere. Tampoco entiendo al torero. Para el torero es también peligroso.

¿Piensas que las corridas de toros son aburridas?

Carlos: No. Esto piensan las personas que no son aficionados, porque no saben. Cada corrida es diferente. Hay toreros con poder, toreros con arte..... siempre hay un sentimiento. Y el toro es también siempre diferente.

María: Sólo veo corridas de toros en la televisión y me horrorizan. Es aburrido porque siempre es lo mismo.

¿Defiendes la prohibición de las corridas de toros?

Carlos: No. Son parte de nuestra cultura y tradición. Pienso que no son negativas para la sociedad.

María: Yo defiendo las asociaciones de defensa de los animales: hacer campañas y concienciar a las personas. Prohibir las corridas no es efectivo. Se pueden hacer ilegalmente. Es mejor hacer campaña, explicar el sufrimiento y la muerte del animal.

(a) According to Carlos, why do people think bullfights are cruel? (1)

(b) What does a fan of the bullfight see when watching? (2)

(c) Again according to Carlos, bullfighting is a cultural activity. What are his reasons for saying this? (4)

(d) Why does Maria think a bullfight is an unequal contest? (1)

(e) She is not in favour of banning bullfighting. Why not? (4)

Minipistas little hints!

Once again we have a fairly long piece of writing but once again you will find that the level of language used is not too difficult (honest!).

- The main thing to remember here is that the passage is divided into a series of questions that reflect the content and order of the questions you are being asked.

- This is made easier for you by having two characters with opposing views. Make sure that you take into account which one is speaking before you attempt to answer the questions.

Question number twenty-four

Here is an article about new regulations affecting people with pets.

Tatuajes, microchips y pasaportes para mascotas de Europa.

Bruselas (Reuters) Perros, gatos y hurones[(1)] que salgan de vacaciones con sus dueños en la Unión Europea tendrán que llevar tatuajes o microchips y un pasaporte de la UE, dijo el jueves la Comisión Europea.

A partir de julio de 2004, las mascotas que viajen de un país a otro de la UE deben llevar un microchip electrónico de identificación, o un tatuaje, y deben haber sido vacunadas contra la rabia.

El pasaporte de la UE para mascotas – con una cubierta azul y estrellas amarillas del emblema europeo – será una prueba de que el animal ha sido vacunado y, opcionalmente, podrá colocarse una fotografía de la mascota.

'La ventaja reside en no tener que averiguar sobre las regulaciones que tiene cada país, de manera que haya una especie de regulación interna para las mascotas viajeras,' dijo la portavoz de la Comisión Beate Gminder en conferencia de prensa.

Muchos turistas dejan ahora a sus mascotas en casa porque las reglamentaciones sobre su admisión varían en cada país, lo que dificulta llevarlas cuando sus dueños viajan.

'Este es un paso significativo para el libre movimiento de personas con sus mascotas y un paso que se ha hecho posible por los grandes avances que hemos logrado en nuestra lucha contra la rabia,' dijo David Byrne, comisionado de Sanidad.

Debido a que no existe la rabia animal en Suecia, Irlanda y Gran Bretaña, esos países mantendrán controles adicionales sobre el ingreso de mascotas hasta el año 2008.

[(1)]*hurones = ferrets*

(a) What control measures on animal travel in the EU will be in place from July 2004?   (3)

(b) Which element of the EU animal passport is optional?   (1)

(c) Why is it difficult at the moment for pet owners to travel with them?   (2)

(d) Why will there be additional controls in Great Britain?   (1)

Minipistas

As with the previous question, this passage gives you good practice in searching for information. The amount of Spanish you need to be able to answer the questions is not huge but, once you have attempted this question as you would in an exam, use it as a source of reading practice and vocabulary.

Answers

1. True

   False

   False

2. the environment

   our future

3. two helpings

   of roast chicken

4. toilets for babies

   space for bulky luggage

   newspapers and magazines

   free parking

5. (a) nocturnal animal

   (b) bite

   (c) stands up

       grinds his teeth

6. 6

   300·000

   5

   4000

7. the cold of the Poles

   a butterfly being born

   how a beehive is organised inside

   the birth of birds in the nest

8. (a) eat all sorts of food

       varied

       in moderation

   (b) have 3-4 meals per day

       follow a regular timetable for meals

   (c) make it more important

   (d) to get a good amount

       you must eat meat and fish

9. to sponsor a child

   to help but not sponsor

   to receive information

10. (a) become a gladiator

        travel the southern seas

        search for marvelous hidden treasure

    (b) put in your stickers

    (c) you will receive prizes

        you will take part in incredible draws

11. (a) that the details of your journey

        match what you asked for

        date of travel

        departure time

    (b) one case

        one piece of hand luggage

        up to 20 kilos in weight

(c) 24 hours for a single ticket

48 hours for a return ticket

12. (a) save space

don't write more than ten lines

(b) don't write too much

express your ideas clearly

(c) a drawing

the better it is

the more chance of getting your letter published

(d) only inside the letter

13. False

True

False

False

14. (a) twenty

(b) a song

(c) a footballer

(d) comfortable clothes

(e) Japanese food

animals

15. (a) by working day and night

(b) weather/atmospheric conditions

(c) observe/obey the traffic signals

drive carefully

16. (a) Henri Desgranges

(b) Eugene Christophe

(c) Anquetil

(d) Raymond Poulidor

(e) Lemond

17. (a) oldest ever discovered

most distant ever discovered

(b) might change theories

about when planets formed

or when life evolved

(c) they were formed millions of years ago

before the sun and its planets.

18. (a) in the morning he trains in the bullring

in the afternoon he goes to school

(b) he says it is his vocation

(c) his father goes with him to the bullring

his mother stays at home and prays

(d) physical preparation

concentration

19. (a) he goes beyond being just a presenter

he introduces humour and irony

about personal details of the competitors

(b) calm their nerves

(c) each round takes a different form

they have only a few seconds to answer questions

20. (a) the courts are very good

the organisers are working very hard (to make everything perfect)

(b) terrible heat

(c) to play in as many tournaments as he can

21. (a) named after friend of his father (a Vietnamese soldier)

(b) 6 months old

imitated dad's swing

when he was shooting balls into a net

(c) both wanted their children to make money

(d) he educated him to be a champion

but only showed him the way to do it

(e) he is his only hero

(f) they have created the 10 commandments according to Tiger

they have set up a 'church'

22. (a) On his first day at school

(b) the teacher was angry

(c) to be a writer

(d) 15 minutes

(e) it's the longest running cartoon series

(f) Groening's dad and son are called Homer

his mother is called Margaret

his sisters are Lisa and Maggie

Bart is an anagram of 'brat'

(g) every programme makes people laugh and think

23. (a) because there's blood

(b) he admires the art/artistry

and the power of the bullfighter

(c) they have continued from generation to generation (for centuries)

they are in literature

they are in painting

many intellectuals are fans

(d) because it's one bull against several men

(e) it wouldn't work

bullfighting would continue illegally

better to campaign

explain the suffering and death of the animal

24. (a) animals must have a microchip

or a tattoo

must have been inoculated against rabies

(b) a photo of the animal

(c) rules on letting them in

are different in every country

(d) they have never had rabies there

Section 4: Writing

The Writing section of the course

Although each of the skills of Speaking, Listening, Reading and Writing is separately assessed for Standard Grade Spanish, they are closely related.

Writing is worth one sixth of your overall mark for the course and it will be assessed by a folio of three pieces of work which should arise from normal class work that you do during your Standard Grade course.

These pieces of Writing could take a number of forms such as:

- short essays

- messages

- letters

- emails

Each of the three pieces of work is equally important. They will be marked individually and awarded a Grade from 1-6 and the final Grade that you get for Writing will be the average of the three.

You will get to practise the pieces of Writing which will go into your folio, drafting and redrafting them after advice from your teacher, but the final version of each must be written up under exam conditions. You will be allowed to use a dictionary for this and, if appropriate to the task, your teacher might supply you with some brief headings to help you. These headings may be in English or in Spanish, so we have given you a mixture of English and Spanish headings. This way, you will have the chance to practise both.

Your Writing can be about anything at all, but the sort of things that you are most likely to be asked to write about are:

- yourself and your family

- where you live

- your school and studies

- your hobbies

- a recent holiday

- your plans for the future

There are no absolute word limits for these pieces of Writing, but at Foundation Level examiners will normally be happy with up to about 50 words for each piece, at General Level, with up to about 100 words and at Credit Level with anything up to about 200 words. But remember it is not the length of your writing that is being assessed but the quality of your Spanish.

Exercise 1 – Writing about yourself

As we said before, the four skills are all linked. So let's begin our preparation for the Writing by looking back at Exercise 1 in the Speaking section on page 45. Let's look at the two versions of Andrew's talk in which he is telling us about himself.

His first version went like this:

> Me llamo Andrew. Tengo 15 años. Vivo en Dundee. En mi familia hay cuatro personas: mi madre, mi padre, mi hermana y yo. Mi madre se llama June y tiene 40 años. Ella es ama de casa. Mi padre se llama David y tiene 42 años. Él es fontanero. Mi hermana se llama Lyndsey y tiene 10 años. Ella está en la escuela primaria. En mi colegio hay 600 estudiantes y 40 profesores. Yo estudio ocho asignaturas. El inglés, las matemáticas, la historia, la química, la física, la música, la informática y el español. En mi tiempo libre me gusta escuchar música, jugar al fútbol e ir a las discotecas el fin de semana.

As a short written text about himself, this would probably be awarded a Grade 3, a good General award. Speaking and Writing at this level are so closely linked that the same basic text will do for both a Speaking and a Writing task.

Look back at pages 45–46, and the advice he was given by his teacher. He was able to improve his talk so that it would get a Credit award and his revised version went like this:

> Hola, me llamo Andrew. Tengo 15 años y vivo en una ciudad en el noreste de Escocia que se llama Dundee. Bueno … Somos cuatro personas en mi familia: mi padre, mi madre, mi hermana y yo. Mi madre, que se llama June, tiene 40 años y es ama de casa. Mi padre, David, tiene 42 años y es fontanero. Me llevo bastante bien con mis padres, pero mi padre es muy estricto. Por eso, me llevo mejor con mi madre. Mi hermana pequeña se llama Lyndsey. Tiene sólo 10 años y está todavía en la escuela primaria. No me llevo bien con ella. Hay siempre disputas en casa, sobre todo cuando yo quiero ver el fútbol en la televisión y ella no. Voy a un colegio grande en el centro de la ciudad. En mi instituto hay más o menos 600 estudiantes y unos 40 profesores. Me gusta bastante el colegio porque tengo muchos amigos allí. Pero tengo mucho trabajo puesto que estudio ocho asignaturas. Las asignaturas que me gustan bastante son el inglés, la historia, la música y la informática. Las que no me gustan son las matemáticas, la química y la física. El español me da igual. Pues, con todo el trabajo que tengo que hacer por el colegio no tengo mucho tiempo libre. Cuando puedo, me gusta escuchar música y jugar al fútbol con mis compañeros. Pero lo que más me gusta es el fin de semana, cuando no hay colegio, salir a la discoteca con mi novia. Lo pasamos bomba.

A lot of the advice about using more complex language, making longer sentences and showing a wider range of vocabulary are equally useful for improving a Writing exercise. There are further changes that we could suggest to this text, however, if it is going to be the basis of a Writing exercise at Credit level.

Can you spot any features of the language used that make this seem like spoken Spanish?

Well, he starts out by saying 'Hola', and he says 'Bueno …' and 'Pues', which are phrases that we use to give ourselves time to think when we are speaking. He also finishes up by saying 'Lo

pasamos bomba', which seems pretty informal in a Writing exercise.

Alright, so those are features of the language which might be improved upon. How does the text look on the page? It is presented as a continuous stream of words! We don't want that in a Writing exercise, do we? We want it to be structured into paragraphs.

Let's see what we can do with this text then, applying two simple techniques:

- make the language slightly more formal

- write in paragraphs

Mi nombre es Andrew Thomson. Tengo 15 años y vivo en una ciudad en el noreste de Escocia que se llama Dundee.

En mi familia hay cuatro personas: mi padre, mi madre, mi hermana y yo. Mi madre, que se llama June, tiene 40 años y es ama de casa. Mi padre, David, tiene 42 años y es fontanero. Me llevo bastante bien con mis padres, pero mi padre es muy estricto. Por eso, me llevo mejor con mi madre. Mi hermana pequeña se llama Lyndsey. Tiene sólo 10 años y está todavía en la escuela primaria. No me llevo bien con ella. Hay siempre disputas en casa, sobre todo cuando yo quiero ver el fútbol en la televisión y ella no.

Voy a un colegio grande en el centro de la ciudad. En mi instituto hay más o menos 600 estudiantes y unos 40 profesores. Me gusta bastante el colegio porque tengo muchos amigos allí. Pero tengo mucho trabajo puesto que estudio ocho asignaturas. Las asignaturas que me gustan bastante son el inglés, la historia, la música y la informática. Las que no me gustan son las matemáticas, la química y la física. El español me da igual.

Desgraciadamente, con todo el trabajo que tengo que hacer por el colegio no tengo mucho tiempo libre. Cuando puedo, me gusta escuchar música y jugar al fútbol con mis compañeros. Pero lo que más me gusta es el fin de semana, cuando no hay colegio, salir a la discoteca con mi novia. Nos encanta esto.

Do you see how simple that was? All he has done is take out the features of spoken language we mentioned earlier, changed a couple of verb forms, introduced his last paragraph by saying 'unfortunately' and given his full name to make his piece of Writing seem a little more formal. This text will now do nicely for a Credit award – if Andrew can write it with this degree of accuracy under exam conditions, using only his dictionary – then he will be awarded a Grade 1 for this piece of work.

Now it's your turn. Look back at the work that you did for Exercise 1 in the Speaking. Re-write your talk as a Writing exercise, making the language a little more formal if possible and structuring it into paragraphs. Use the following headings to help you:

- información personal (nombre, edad, residencia)

- familia (personas, actitudes)

- colegio (asignaturas, opiniones)

- tiempo libre (actividades, gustos)

Once you have drafted your piece of Writing, you might find is useful to show it to your teacher so that he/she can point out any problems that you may have had with the language. You can then practise re-writing this piece, using only your dictionary and the headings given here.

Useful words and phrases

Look at the changes Andrew had to make, both to improve his talk and to improve his writing. Most of the words he added were either connecting words which helped him make longer sentences, or adverbs, which told us more about where, when or how things were done, or phrases which helped to structure what he was saying/writing. Here are a some useful words and phrases of this type that you can use to improve your Spanish:

Adverbs, connecting words and structuring phrases

- y   *and*
- que   *which/that/who*
- porque   *because*
- para   *in order to*
- visto que   *since*
- puesto que   *since*
- cuando   *when*
- como   *how*
- desgraciadamente   *unfortunately*
- por desgracia   *unfortunately*
- sólo   *only*
- todavía   *still*
- primero   *firstly*
- por primero   *firstly*
- en primer lugar   *firstly*
- segundo   *secondly*
- en segundo lugar   *secondly*
- tercero   *thirdly*
- en tercer lugar   *thirdly*
- entonces   *then*
- luego   *then*
- después   *afterwards*
- antes ... después ...   *before ... after ...*
- antes ... ahora ...   *previously ... now ...*
- de vez en cuando   *sometimes*
- por eso   *for this reason*
- a mi modo de ver   *in my opinion*
- para mí   *as far as I am concerned*
- al final   *finally*
- al fin y al cabo   *at the end of the day*
- para terminar   *in conclusion*
- para concluir   *in conclusion*

Exercise 2

Make a note of these phrases and add others to your list as you come across them during your Standard Grade course.

Exercise 3 – Short essay about plans for the future

Here are some of the key points to remember whenever you write an essay in Spanish:

- Plan your essay well – make sure you have an introduction and a conclusion.

- Try to express opinions and feelings – don't just give lists.

- Try to find ways to show off your best Spanish – don't just stick to very simple things.

- Be careful with your grammar – after you have finished writing, check your work thoroughly

Keeping these points in mind, write an essay about your plans for the future.

Think about ways to talk about the future in Spanish. Here are a few expressions that might help you:

- Si apruebo los exámenes, quiero estudiar ... el año que viene.

  If I pass my exams, I want to study ... next year.

- Al terminar el colegio, espero continuar mis estudios en ...

  When I finish school, I hope to carry on studying at ...

- Pienso estudiar ...

  I intend to study ...

- Cuando sea mayor ...

  When I am grown up ...

- Quiero ser ...

  I want to be ...

- Voy a trabajar de ...

  I'm going to work as ...

- Trabajaré en ...

  I will work in ...

- Me gustaría vivir en ...

  I would like to live in ...

Before you start writing your essay, think about the sort of things that you would like to write about. These might include:

- what you are doing this year at school

- how you think you might get on in your exams

- what you would like to do next year

- whether you would like to go to college or university

- what sort of job you would like to do

- your longer term goals: home? marriage? family?

You could use these suggestions to help you plan your essay. You could also use some of the adverbs, connecting words and structuring phrases which we gave you earlier (page 103) to help you put it all together.

Now, try writing your essay, using the six bullet points above as headings.

When you have written your essay, show it to your teacher or another Spanish speaker and ask for their advice on how to improve it.

(In the answer key at the end of this section, on page 110, we've given you an example of an essay about future plans. You might be able to use this for some ideas on how to improve your own work.

Exercise 4 – Writing a letter

An important type of Writing that you might wish to practise for your folio is Letter Writing.

When you write a letter in Spanish, there are two important points to bear in mind:

- layout
- set phrases

Let's look at each of these in turn.

The traditional way to set out a letter in Spanish is to have your address at the top left hand side of the page, the address of the person you are writing to just below that on the right hand side of the page and the date and place you are writing from, just below that again on the left hand side of the page. Let's look at an example.

Andrew Thomson
40 Pollock Road
Dundee
DD1 2AB

> Juan García Fernández
> Cuesta de Alpacete, 47
> 04100 – Barcelona

Dundee, 12 de febrero de 2004

Querido Juan,

Nowadays, with so many letters being written on computers, it is becoming quite common to see letters in Spanish with everything at the left hand side of the page. In this case, the address of the person you are writing to comes first, then the place and date you are writing from and then, right at the end of the letter, your own name and address. This layout for a letter looks like this:

Juan García Fernández
Cuesta de Alpacete, 47
04100 – Barcelona

Dundee, 12 de febrero de 2004

Querido Juan,

Text of the letter

Un abrazo,

Andrew

Andrew Thomson
40 Pollock Road
Dundee
DD1 2AB

In this second example we have given the two most important phrases you need to write a letter of this type in Spanish. Start the letter by saying:

Querido/querida

followed by the name of the person you are writing to. End the letter by saying:

Un abrazo

followed by your own name.

Useful words and phrases for letters

Here are some other words and phrases that might be useful to you when you are writing letters:

- (Muchas) gracias por tu carta — *Thank you (very much) for your letter*
- He recibido tu carta esta mañana — *I got your letter this morning*
- Discúlpame por no haber escrito antes pero ... — *I'm sorry I haven't written sooner but ...*
- Nada más por ahora — *That's all for now*
- Escríbeme pronto — *Write to me soon*

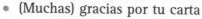

Pista

In addition to learning these phrases, you might want to write them down in a notebook to help you remember them. Remember, these are just examples, so leave enough space under each heading to write in more examples that you will come across during your Standard Grade Spanish course.

Now, let's try some practice in writing a letter. Take a look at the text that you wrote for Exercise 1 in this section. Suppose you wanted to write a letter introducing yourself to a Spanish pupil from a school with which your school was setting up an exchange. Could you just drop this text into a letter format and leave it at that? No! That's right, what is missing? I'm sure you have guessed – questions! The text we wrote for Exercise 1 was just to give information, but when we write a letter to someone to introduce ourselves, we ask for information too.

Look back at the Listening Section (pages 11–13) where we looked at question words. Here are some questions that you might want to add to your text from Exercise 1 to make it more of a letter:

- ¿Cuántos años tienes?
- ¿Cuántas personas hay en tu familia?
- ¿A qué se dedican tus padres?
- ¿En qué trabaja tu padre?
- ¿Tienes hermanos?
- ¿Cómo es tu colegio?
- ¿Cuántos estudiantes hay en tu colegio?
- ¿Te caen simpáticos los profesores?
- ¿Cuántas asignaturas estudias?
- ¿Qué asignatura te gusta más?
- ¿Tienes una asignatura favorita?
- ¿Qué te gusta hacer en tu tiempo libre?
- ¿Qué te gusta hacer los fines de semana?

We haven't given you the English for any of these, but we're sure you'll recognise many of them. If not, you can always use your dictionary to find out what they mean.

Now, try re-writing the text that you prepared for Exercise 1, using a letter format and using some of these questions to make it seem more like a letter. Remember, you don't have to use them all – that would make your letter too long.

(In the answer key at the end of this section, we've given you an example of what Andrew's text might look like written up as a letter using some of these phrases.)

Exercise 5 – Writing a short message

Now we are going to look at how you might write a short message in Spanish. This is a more straightforward type of writing than those we have seen in Exercises 1, 3 and 4. If you are going to do this sort of writing, you will probably be given **very clear instructions** about what you have to write.

Follow these three simple pieces of advice, and you should have no problem with this type of exercise:

1. Give all of the details you are asked to give.

2. Try to keep your Spanish simple and straightforward.

3. Make sure that you check it carefully so that there aren't any silly mistakes!

Now, have a go at this exercise:

Imagine you are staying with your pen friend in Spain and you have answered the phone while he/she is out. Write a message telling her/him that:

- Her/his aunt called.
- She will be late as her train was delayed.
- She will be on her own as her/his uncle had to work.
- She will arrive at about half past nine.
- No-one will have to go and get her.
- She will get a taxi from the station.

(In the answer key at the end of this section, we've given you an example of what this message might look like. The example we give is about fifty words long, and it is the sort of writing exercise that would be awarded a good General mark.)

Minipistas little hints!

- You might want to use past and future tenses in this note, make sure you check the spelling of any verbs that you use – be particularly careful about the accents: miss an accent and you can completely change the meaning of what you are saying!

Exercise 6 – Writing an email

Writing an email is a lot easier than writing a letter as you don't normally have to worry about the layout. It is more like the message writing that we saw in Exercise 5 than the letter writing in Exercise 4.

Look back at the advice you were given for Exercise 5, and then try this exercise.

Write an email to your exchange partner in a Spanish school telling her/him:

- The information that she/he sent about her/his school has arrived

- Thank her/him for it.

- Tell him/her what you think of it

- Ask if she/he has got the information that you sent

- Tell her/him it is very interesting

- Tell her/him you can't wait to meet in June.

(In the answer key at the end of this section, we've given you an example of what this message might look like. The example we give is about fifty words long, and it is the sort of writing exercise that would be awarded a good General mark.)

Exercise 7 – Short essay about a holiday

Here are some of the key points to remember from Exercises 1, 3 and 4:

- Prepare your essay well.

- Plan how to structure it.

- Show off your best Spanish by not just sticking to very simple things.

- Try to make your Spanish grammatically accurate – after you have finished writing, check your work thoroughly.

Keeping these points in mind, what you are going to do now is **prepare a short essay about a holiday.**

Before you start, think about the sort of things that you will want to say, these might include:

- Where you went

- How you got there

- How long you were there

- Something about the weather

- Something about things you did like cinema, theatre, museums, sports, discos.

You might well know most of these things anyway, but can you think of any way of getting this information in Spanish? Why not take a look through the various vocabulary notes and the Reading section in this book. You'll find lots of words and phrases that will be useful for this type of essay. If you can't find what you are looking for, you can always use your dictionary to find any more that you may need.

Here are some headings in Spanish that might help you to write your essay:

- Las vacaciones del año pasado (¿cuándo? ¿dónde?)
- El viaje (¿cómo?)
- La estancia (¿cuánto duró? ¿cómo?)
- El tiempo (¿cómo?)
- Las actividades (¿la gente? ¿la playa? ¿el cine? ¿las discotecas? ¿los monumentos?)
- Opiniones/impresiones (¿qué te gustó? ¿qué no te gustó?)

When you have written your essay, you might like to try showing it to your teacher or another Spanish speaker and see if they have any advice to give you on how to improve it.

Then you can practise re-writing it using just your headings to help you prepare for writing up your folio pieces.

(In the answer key at the end of this section, we've given you an example of an essay about a holiday. You might be able to use this for some ideas on how to improve your essay.)

Exercise 8 – Short report on work experience

As we said earlier, you will be doing some activities related to the world of work during your Standard Grade Spanish course.

For this exercise, we'd like you to **write a short report about your work experience**. If you haven't done your work experience yet, or if you won't be doing work experience, you could use the information from Exercise 5 in the Speaking section (page 49) to give you something to write about.

Before you begin, look over the notes for the previous exercises in this section about preparing for Writing exercises. Now try writing about your work experience using the following headings:

- Experiencia del trabajo (¿cuándo? ¿dónde?)
- Horario del trabajo
- Actividades principales (¿cuáles?)
- Los colegas (¿cómo eran?)
- Opiniones/impresiones (¿qué te gustó? ¿qué no te gustó?)

When you have written your essay, you might like to try showing it to your teacher or another Spanish speaker and see if they have any advice to give you on how to improve it.

(In the answer key at the end of this section, we've given you an example of a report based on Exercise 5 from the Speaking section. You might be able to use this for some ideas on how to improve your report.)

Answer key to the Writing exercises

Exercise 3 – Short essay about plans for the future

Éste es un año muy importante para mí. Estoy en cuarto y estudio ocho asignaturas a nivel de Standard Grade. En mayo tengo los exámenes y, si los apruebo, quiero volver al colegio el año que viene para continuar mis estudios.

Espero estudiar cinco asignaturas a nivel de Higher porque me gustaría ir a la universidad para estudiar las ciencias políticas. Por eso, tengo que seguir estudiando los estudios contemporáneos, mi asignatura favorita, y el inglés, pero no sé qué otras asignaturas estudiaré en quinto.

Si consigo una plaza en la universidad, estaré cuatro años allí.

Al terminar mis estudios en la universidad, quiero trabajar de periodista porque me parece muy interesante y me encanta viajar.

Más allá en el futuro, quiero casarme, tener cuatro hijos y vivir en una casa muy bonita en el sur de España.

Exercise 4 – Writing a letter

Juan García Fernández
Cuesta de Alpacete, 47
04100 – Barcelona

Dundee, 12 de febrero de 2004

Querido Juan,

Mi nombre es Andrew Thomson. Tengo 15 años y vivo en una ciudad en el noreste de Escocia que se llama Dundee.

¿Cuántas personas hay en tu familia? En mi familia hay cuatro personas: mi padre, mi madre, mi hermana y yo. Mi madre, que se llama June, tiene 40 años y es ama de casa. Mi padre, David, tiene 42 años y es fontanero. Me llevo bastante bien con mis padres, pero mi padre es muy estricto. Por eso, me llevo mejor con mi madre.

¿Tienes hermanos? Yo tengo una hermana pequeña que se llama Lyndsey. Tiene sólo 10 años y está todavía en la escuela primaria. No me llevo bien con ella. Hay siempre disputas en casa, sobre todo cuando yo quiero ver el fútbol en la televisión y ella no.

Voy a un colegio grande en el centro de la ciudad. En mi instituto hay más o menos 600 estudiantes y unos 40 profesores. Me gusta bastante el colegio porque tengo muchos amigos allí. ¿Cómo es tu colegio? ¿Cuántos estudiantes hay? ¿Te caen simpáticos los profesores?

Tengo mucho trabajo en el colegio, puesto que estudio ocho asignaturas. Las asignaturas que me gustan bastante son el inglés, la historia, la música y la informática. Las que no me gustan son las matemáticas, la química y la física. El español me da igual. ¿Cuántas asignaturas estudias? ¿Tienes una asignatura favorita?

continued ...

¿Qué te gusta hacer en tu tiempo libre? Desgraciadamente, con todo el trabajo que tengo que hacer por el colegio no tengo mucho tiempo libre. Cuando puedo, me gusta escuchar música y jugar al fútbol con mis compañeros. Pero lo que más me gusta es el fin de semana, salir a la discoteca con mi novia.

Tengo que acabar mi carta ahora. Escríbeme pronto.

Un abrazo,

Andrew

Andrew Thomson
40 Pollock Road
Dundee
DD1 2AB

Exercise 5 – Writing a short message

Victoria,

Tu tía llamó por teléfono. Llegará tarde porque su tren salió con retraso. Estará aquí sobre las nueve y media. Cogerá un taxi, así que nadie tiene que ir a la estación para buscarla.

Lauren

Exercise 6 – Writing an email

Jaime,

Acabo de recibir la información que enviaste sobre tu colegio. Gracias por eso. Parece muy interesante. No sabía que tu colegio tiene mil doscientos alumnos. ¿Recibiste la información que te enviamos sobre nuestro instituto? No puedo esperar el mes de junio para conocerte de persona.

Richard

Exercise 7 – Short essay about a holiday

El año pasado fui de vacaciones a España con mi familia. Pasamos dos semanas en un hotel en Benidorm, mis padres, mi hermano y yo.

El viaje era bastante difícil. Fuimos en coche hasta el aeropuerto de Prestwick para coger el vuelo para Alicante. Por desgracia, hubo un retraso de cuatro horas. ¡Qué lío!

Pero al llegar a Benidorm todo era fenomenal. Mis padres pasaban todo el día en el hotel – o en el bar o en la piscina – así que mi hermano y yo estábamos libres para hacer lo que queríamos.

Ibamos a la playa cada mañana para nadar y tomar el sol.

Al mediodía, hacía siempre mucho calor así que, por la tarde, íbamos de paseo por el centro comercial y conocimos a unos chicos irlandeses que estaban de vacaciones allí. Se llamaban Liam y Declan y eran muy simpáticos.

Por la noche, salíamos con los nuevos amigos irlandeses a la discoteca después de cenar y no volvíamos al hotel hasta las dos o las tres de la madrugada.

Eran unas vacaciones estupendas. Lo que más me gustó era salir a la discoteca cada noche y lo que menos me gustó era el calor del mediodía.

Al fin y al cabo, quiero volver allí el año que viene – pero sin mis padres.

Exercise 8 – Short report on work experience

En febrero de este año, pasé una semana trabajando en una oficina en el centro de Glasgow. Se trataba de la oficina de una agencia de publicidad. Mi tío es diseñador allí y por eso tuve la posibilidad de trabajar en su compañía.

El horario de trabajo era flexible, así que llegaba cada mañana entre las ocho y media y las nueve y media y salía del trabajo cada tarde entre las cuatro y media y las cinco y media. Tenía un cuarto de hora de descanso por la mañana, y otro cuarto de hora por la tarde. Al mediodía, tenía una hora libre para comer.

Durante la jornada, yo tenía que distribuir el correo, sacar fotocopias, contestar el teléfono y confirmar citas con los clientes de la agencia.

Me gustó bastante el trabajo, pero era algo aburrido. Al final de la semana, los colegas me regalaron un CD. Eran muy simpáticos.

A fin de cuentas, era una experiencia muy buena para mí. Aprendí algo sobre cómo funciona el mundo de la publicidad pero, sober todo, aprendí que no quiero trabajar en una oficina al dejar el colegio. Quiero ir a la universidad y seguir estudiando. Es más fácil.

Section 5: Grammar

Grammar – how Spanish works!

In addition to learning all of the set phrases we have given you in the previous sections of this book, it is well worth studying the grammar given here. If you've ever tried to play a board game like *Monopoly* or *Cluedo* without knowing the rules you'll know how confusing this can be and learning a foreign language is no different.

We don't suggest that you learn the things that we tell you here just as rules. The important thing is that, if you understand them, you will be able to use them when you speak or write Spanish to make up your own new phrases and sentences. This is very important for both your Speaking and Writing. It is also important if you want to take your Spanish further, by going on to Higher, for example.

Remember, the information that we give you about grammar is just a starting point and if you do carry on with Spanish, you'll find that there is a lot more where this came from.

Nouns and articles

All Spanish nouns are described as belonging to one of two groups. They are either masculine or feminine and this distinction is known as gender. This is important, because the Spanish language works quite differently from English, and words will change in ways which show the relationships between them much more clearly than in English.

Most nouns which end in '**–o**' are masculine, for example:

> el piso   el chico   el aspecto

although two very common ones are feminine:

> la mano   la radio

Most nouns which end in '**–a**' are feminine, for example:

> la casa   la geografía   la pista

although some very common ones are masculine, for example:

> el idioma   el problema   el sistema

When nouns don't end in either '**–o**' or '**–a**' it can be more difficult to tell if they are masculine or feminine although words for males are almost always masculine, for example:

> el padre   el hombre

and those for females are almost always feminine, for example:

> la madre   la mujer

You will see from the examples that we have given that the word for 'the' with masculine nouns is '**el**' and with feminine nouns is '**la**'. When nouns are plural, these words change.

We make Spanish nouns plural by adding an '**–s**' if they end in a vowel and an '**–es**' if they end in a consonant, for example:

> chicos   asignaturas   señores   ciudades

Pista

Whenever you learn a new word, learn it along with the *artículo definido* – the word for 'the' – so that you will remember what gender it is. If you check your dictionary, you'll find that it always shows whether a noun is masculine or feminine, usually by giving (m) or (f) in the entry.

The article also changes to '**los**' or '**las**', so in these cases we would have:

los chicos   las asignaturas   los señores   las ciudades

It is also important to know the indefinite article or word for 'a/some'. This is '**un**' with a masculine noun and '**una**' with a feminine noun, and the two plural forms are '**unos**' and '**unas**'. For example:

un amigo   una amiga   unos amigos   unas amigas

Adjectives

As we said earlier, Spanish words group together to show relationships between them. This is particularly important with adjectives which describe nouns. Adjectives will always match up with the noun that they are describing in number and gender.

That means that most adjectives in Spanish will have four forms, for example:

pequeño   pequeña   pequeños   pequeñas

The form that you use will depend on the noun you are describing so you will say:

el hermano pequeño

la mesa pequeña

los bebés pequeños

las salas pequeñas

Notice the way in which the words in each of these groups are all **agreeing** with each other or matching up. They are forming little groups which show that the words are related in some way.

When the basic form of an adjective does not end in an '**-o**', it will usually only have two forms, singular and plural, for example:

azul   azules   interesante   interesantes

and so you will say:

el libro azul

las pelotas azules

la historia interesante

los ejercicios interesantes

Exercise 1

Complete the following sentences with the appropriate form of the adjective in brackets.

1. La piscina está en un palacio .... en el centro de la ciudad. (antiguo)

2. El inglés es mi asignatura .... (favorito)

3. No todos los profesores son .... (divertido)

4. Estos exámenes son .... (importante)

5. Mi hermana es muy .... (ágil)

Pista

The words which tell you who something belongs to in Spanish are adjectives. That is why words like my (mi) or your (tu/vuestro) or his/her/their (su) will change depending on whether the thing owned is singular or plural, masculine or feminine – e.g. mi cuaderno but mis padres; tu casa but tus ejercicios; nuestro amigo but nuestras asignaturas etc.

Pronouns

One important aspect of any language is the way in which you can miss things out, or replace things with something shorter, without losing any of the meaning. Think about your early days at school when you were asked to write a story. How much better was it if you did not constantly repeat the name of the main character but occasionally replaced the name with 'he' or 'she', 'him' or 'her'?

Words which let you do this are called **pronouns**. These are words which can stand in for nouns, and that is how they get their name.

To make it easy to learn the pronouns which you have come across in the set phrases throughout this book, they can be grouped together according to how you use them.

When pronouns are grouped together like this they are normally in this order:

	singular	plural
1st	I/me	we/us
2nd	you	you (plural)
3rd	he/she/it/him/her	they/them

These are sometimes referred to as the 'six persons' and usually described as first, second and third singular, and first, second and third plural, as shown in the table.

Subject pronouns

	singular	plural
1st	yo	nosotros/nosotras
2nd	tú	vosotros/vosotras
3rd	él/ella/Vd (usted)	ellos/ellas/Vds (ustedes)

Subject pronouns can stand in for a noun which is **doing** the action in a sentence. For example:

> **Las chicas** están en el aula. **Ellas** están en el aula.
> *The girls are in the classroom. They are in the classroom.*

> **Mi padre** y yo fuimos al estadio. **Nosotros** fuimos al estadio.
> *My father and I went to the stadium. We went to the stadium.*

You should know, however, that in Spanish these pronouns are often missed out altogether. The reason for this is quite simple – in most cases the endings of verbs already tell you who is doing a particular action. Pronouns do help, however, whenever there is confusion – for example, if you need to know whether it is a 'he' or a 'she' who is the subject. There may also be cases in which you wish to put a strong emphasis on the person doing the action.

Compare the following:

> Arreglé mi dormitorio.
> *I tidied up my room.*

but

¿Quién arregló el dormitorio? Lo arreglé yo.
Who tidied up the room? I tidied it.

Look back at the examples given on the previous page. Which of these could be written without a pronoun at all?

> ### Pista Tip
>
> - In Spanish, there are two ways of calling someone 'you'. The one we use most in this book is the form '**tú**', which is called the familiar form. There is also the polite form of address '**usted**' - often written as the abbreviation '**Vd**'. Nowadays, except in formal settings, such as going through customs or checking in at hotels, it is quite acceptable to use '**tú**' most of the time. Apart from a few set phrases which use the polite form, we have used the informal form throughout this book.

Direct object pronouns

	singular	plural
1st	me	nos
2nd	te	os
3rd	lo/la/se	los/las/se

These can stand in for a person or thing which is having something **directly** done to it in a sentence. For example:

Leo **el libro**. Lo leo.
I read the book. I read it.

Vemos **la televisión**. La vemos.
We watch television. We watch it.

Indirect object pronouns

	singular	plural
1st	me	nos
2nd	te	os
3rd	le/se	les/se

These can stand in for a person or thing which is having something indirectly done to it in a sentence. For example:

Doy los libros **a los profesores**. Les doy los libros.
I give the books to the teachers. I give the books to them.

Envío la carta **a mi amiga colombiana**. Le envío la carta.
I send the letter to my Colombian friend. I send the letter to her.

Notice that the direct and indirect object pronouns are being placed right in front of the verb in these examples. Remember what we said about Spanish words grouping together to show how they are related to each other? In this case the position tells you about the relationship too!

> **Pista** | **Tip**
>
> • Sometimes you can make your Spanish even more impressive by missing out two things in a sentence and using two object pronouns together. If you want to do this always remember to put the indirect object pronoun **before** the direct object pronoun and to change '**le**' or '**les**' to '**se**'. If you look at the last two examples you can see that we could make them even shorter by saying '**Se lo doy**' – *I give it to him* and '**Se la envío**' – *I send it to her.*

Strong pronouns

	singular	plural
1st	mí	nosotros/nosotras
2nd	ti	vosotros/vosotras
3rd	él/ella/sí	ellos/ellas/sí

These are usually found after a preposition like **for**, **with**, **against**, etc.

For example:

El regalo es **para mi madre**. El regalo es para **ella**.
The present is for my mother. The present is for her.

Estuvimos en la fiesta con **los chicos peruanos**. Estuvimos en la fiesta con **ellos**.
We were at the party with the Peruvian boys. We were at the party with them.

Exercise 2

Re-write the following sentences, replacing the words underlined with pronouns.

1. <u>Los padres de Antonio</u> son de España.

2. <u>La hermana de Angela</u> está en mi clase.

3. Preparan <u>la comida</u> antes de salir.

4. Victoria pone <u>los bolis</u> en la mesa.

5. Jaime bebe <u>el café</u>.

6. Ofrezco los billetes <u>a mis amigos</u>.

7. El profesor explica el problema <u>a mi padre</u>.

8. Damos <u>el dinero al conductor</u>.

9. Los libros nuevos son para <u>los estudiantes españoles</u>.

10. Llamaron por <u>su prima</u>.

Verbs

Verbs are the part of the Spanish language which give most trouble to English speakers learning Spanish.

This is because in Spanish the form of the verb carries more information than in English.

Firstly, the verb in Spanish tells you **who** is doing something.

In addition to indicating **who** is doing something, it will also give us information about the **time setting** of the action. This information about the time setting of an action is normally referred to as **tense**.

This additional information is usually conveyed by changing the ending of the verb, which means the same basic word can have dozens of different forms. That doesn't happen in English and, at first, we can find this very difficult.

It isn't really that difficult, though, as these different forms almost always follow set patterns. Master a few basic patterns and you should have no trouble.

Verbs in Spanish tend to be referred to by the part known as the **infinitive** and, depending on whether this ends in '**–ar**', '**–er**' or '**–ir**', they are considered as belonging to one of **Three Groups**. The most common way that verbs change is to take off the last two letters of the infinitive and add different endings.

Look back at what we said about sets of pronouns on page 116. The forms of a Spanish verb are normally given in sets of six parts too and these parts follow the same order as the sets of pronouns.

Pista

This means that you normally don't need to use a pronoun with a Spanish verb.

The present tense

The most important tense in Spanish is called the Present tense. This tense which is used to talk about what is happening now or to make general statements of fact (I am going to the shops. In Scotland it rains a lot.) is one of the most commonly used in everyday Spanish. The vast majority of Spanish verbs in this tense follow the same basic patterns.

	singular	plural
1st	hablo	hablamos
2nd	hablas	habláis
3rd	habla	hablan

Regular verbs ending in '**–ar**', like '**hablar**', follow this pattern in the present tense:

Those ending in '**–er**', such as '**vender**', follow a similar pattern, with an '**e**' replacing the '**a**' we saw in the first group.

	singular	plural
1st	vendo	vendemos
2nd	vendes	vendéis
3rd	vende	venden

Those ending in '**–ir**' follow the pattern that we see here in '**vivir**':

	singular	plural
1st	vivo	vivimos
2nd	vives	vivís
3rd	vive	viven

The following is a list of common regular verbs which follow these patterns.

Pista

Watch out for regular '–er' and '–ir' verbs which end in '–cer' or '–cir'. The first person of these verbs is written with a 'zc'. So 'conocer' gives us 'conozco' and 'producir' gives us 'produzco'.

> **AR verbs:**
>
> bajar buscar cambiar cantar charlar cortar cruzar cuidar dejar descansar enseñar escuchar esperar firmar ganar gastar indicar iniciar limpiar llegar llenar llevar mejorar nadar sacar terminar
>
> **ER verbs:**
>
> aprender beber comer comprender correr creer leer vender
>
> **IR verbs:**
>
> abrir escribir cubrir decidir

(Remember to look these up and note the meanings.)

As you might guess from looking at these lists, the AR verbs are by far the biggest group.

Exercise 3

Complete the sentences with the appropriate form of the present tense of the verb in brackets.

1. La profesora .... cuatro idiomas. (hablar)

2. En Benidorm, nosotros siempre .... en el mismo restaurante chino. (comer)

3. Los abuelos de mi compañero español .... cerca de Barcelona. (vivir)

4. Durante las vacaciones, yo .... cada día en el mar. (nadar)

5. ¿ .... tú un intercambio con un chico escocés? (buscar)

Why not try to write down in English the meaning of these sentences?

Ser and estar

Some verbs do not follow these patterns and are generally referred to as **irregular verbs**. The verbs '**ser**' and '**estar**' are two or the most important irregular verbs in Spanish and they have the following forms:

Ser	singular	plural
1st	soy	somos
2nd	eres	sois
3rd	es	son

Estar	singular	plural
1st	estoy	estamos
2nd	estás	estáis
3rd	está	están

These are the first two verbs that we have come across where the first person does not end in '**–o**'. Notice that, other than this, and the written accents on some of its parts, the verb '**estar**' is very similar to the regular verbs ending in '**–ar**' in this tense.

These two verbs both mean 'to be', but they are used quite differently from each other. This can sometimes be confusing for English speakers, but if you can master a few simple rules, there is no reason why it should be.

Ser

a. We use '**ser**' to link together two nouns (or noun phrases – including numbers and pronouns) to identify who or what someone or something is. So we say:

> Mis padres son profesores.
> *My parents are teachers.*

> Los dos son profesores.
> *The two of them are teachers.*

> Ellos son profesores.
> *They are teachers.*

b. With adjectives, we also use '**ser**' if we are describing an essential quality of something – like its size, shape, colour, what it is made of, or, with people, their nationality, what they look like or personality traits. For example:

> El libro es azul.
> *The book is blue.*

> Mis hermanas son bajas y morenas.
> *My sisters are small and dark.*

> Nuestros abuelos son irlandeses.
> *Our grandparents are Irish.*

c. We also use '**ser**' in impersonal expressions like, 'It is necessary', or 'It is important', for example:

> Es importante cruzar la calle aquí.
> *It is important to cross the road here.*

> Es necesario comprar los billetes antes.
> *It is necessary to buy the tickets first.*

Estar

a. We use '**estar**', on the other hand, to say where something is located:

> Zaragoza está en España. *Zaragoza is in Spain.*
> Los libros están sobre la mesa. *The books are on the table.*

Pista

When you want to say 'There is ...', or 'There are ...' use the form 'hay'. For example 'Hay muchos cines en Glasgow'. There are lots of cinemas in Glasgow.

b. With adjectives, we use **'estar'** to describe the state or condition that something is in. For example:

> La ventana está rota.
> *The window is broken.*

> Los niños están enfermos.
> *The children are ill.*

c. Another important use of **'estar'** is to form the continuous tenses. (I am doing, we are waiting, etc.) To do this, we need a form of the verb called the gerund ending in **'–ando'** for **'–ar'** verbs, and in **'–iendo'** for **'–er'** or **'–ir'** verbs. For example:

> hablar – hablando (*speaking*)

> comer – comiendo (*eating*)

> vivir – viviendo (*living*)

We use **'estar'** with these verb forms to emphasise what is (or was) going on **right at the time we are talking about**. So we could say:

> De momento estoy estudiando español.
> *At the moment, I am studying Spanish.*

> Durante todo el viaje de regreso los alumnos estaban charlando.
> *During the whole of the journey back the pupils were chatting.*

Exercise 4

Complete the sentences by choosing the appropriate form of **'ser'** or **'estar'**.

1. Mi madre .... de Venezuela. (es/está)

2. Las fuentes .... en la Plaza de España. (son/están)

3. No podemos ir al colegio porque .... resfríados. (somos/estamos)

4. La física .... una asignatura difícil. (es/está)

5. .... muy preocupado a causa de mis estudios. (soy/estoy)

Gustar

We say what we like in Spanish by using the verb **'gustar'**:

> Me gusta la comida china.
> *I like Chinese food.*

> Me gusta ver la televisión.
> *I like watching television.*

> Me gustan las películas de Penélope Cruz.
> *I like the films of Penélope Cruz.*

'Gustar' is a **regular verb**, but notice that when the thing we like is singular, or an activity expressed by another verb, then we say **'me gusta'** but, when the thing we like is plural, we say **'me gustan'**. We are literally saying something like, 'Chinese food is pleasing to me', 'Watching television is pleasing to me', or 'The films of Penélope Cruz are pleasing to me'!

There are a few other verbs in Spanish that work like this with pronouns. The most common ones are '**encantar**', '**interesar**', '**parecer**' and '**dar**', in the expressions '**dar asco**' and '**dar igual**'. For example:

> Me encanta el teatro.
> *I really like the theatre.*

> Nos interesan los tebeos americanos.
> *We are interested in American comics.*

> ¿Qué te parece la comida india?
> *What do you think of Indian food?*

> Les da asco estudiar.
> *They hate studying.*

> Me da igual viajar en avión.
> *I don't mind travelling by plane.*

Reflexive verbs

In addition to these, there is another important group of verbs which we use with a pronoun in expressions like:

> Me llamo Ian McIntosh.
> *My name is Ian McIntosh.*

This is what is generally known as a reflexive verb in Spanish. This means a verb which has the same **subject** and **object**. Think of a man looking into a mirror – what does he see? That's right – a reflection of himself. Reflexive verbs are often recognisable in English by the word 'self' – myself, yourself, himself, etc. The expression '**Me llamo**' literally means 'I call myself'.

Many everyday activities in Spanish are expressed by using verbs of this type:

> **Me despierto** a las 7 de la mañana.
> *I wake up at seven in the morning.*

> Mis hermanos **se levantan** a las 8 y media.
> *My brothers get up at half past eight.*

> **Se duchan** y **se limpian** los dientes antes de **marcharse** para el colegio.
> *They shower and brush their teeth before setting out for school.*

> Siempre **te vistes** muy elegante.
> *You always dress very elegantly.*

> **Nos despedimos** del profesor al acabar la clase.
> *We say goodbye to the teacher at the end of the class.*

> ¿A qué hora **os acostáis** los fines de semana?
> *What time do you go to bed at the weekend?*

> El bebé **se duerme** muy temprano.
> *The baby goes to sleep very early.*

As you can see, when we write out the various part of the verb, the pronouns '**me**', '**te**', '**se**', '**nos**', '**os**' and '**se**' are placed in front of the verb. With the infinitive these pronouns are attached to the verb and written as a single word.

> Voy a marcharme a las ocho.
> *I'm going to leave at eight o'clock.*
>
> Quieren ducharse antes de salir.
> *They want to have a shower before going out.*

Radical changing verbs

Some of the verbs given above are a bit strange. Look at the following patterns:

despertar	singular	plural
1st	despierto	despertamos
2nd	despiertas	despertáis
3rd	despierta	despiertan

pedir	singular	plural
1st	pido	pedimos
2nd	pides	pedís
3rd	pide	piden

dormir	singular	plural
1st	duermo	dormimos
2nd	duermes	dormís
3rd	duerme	duermen

acostarse	singular	plural
1st	me acuesto	nos acostamos
2nd	te acuestas	os acostáis
3rd	se acuesta	se acuestan

Pista

Look at the way we have laid these verbs out in tables. The parts that change are in the shape of an 'L'. This might help you to remember them!

You will notice that in the first, second and third person singular and in the third person plural the vowel sound is different from that in the infinitive and in the other two parts. The reason for this is that the main stress in these parts of the verb is on the stem, (the bit that's left when you take away the '**ar**', '**er**' or '**ir**'!) and in the others it is on the ending.

In some cases, (eg. '**despertar**') an '**e**' in the infinitive changes to '**ie**'. In some '**ir**' verbs, (eg. '**pedir**') '**e**' becomes '**i**'. In other cases, '**o**' changes to '**ue**'.

• acostar	*to lie down*	acuesto, etc.
• cerrar	*to close*	cierro, etc.
• comenzar	*to start*	comienzo, etc.
• contar	*to count/tell a story*	cuento, etc.
• costar	*to cost*	cuesto, etc.
• defender	*to defend*	defiendo, etc.
• descender	*to go down*	desciendo, etc.
• despertar	*to awake*	despierto, etc.
• divertir	*to amuse*	divierto, etc.
• encontrar	*to find/meet*	encuentro, etc.
• entender	*to understand*	entiendo, etc.
• morir	*to die*	muero, etc.
• mostrar	*to show*	muestro, etc.
• pedir	*to request*	pido, etc.

Pista

Watch out for the verb 'jugar', to play. This verb changes like 'acostarse', but it is the 'u' that changes to 'ue'.

perder	to lose	pierdo, etc.
preferir	to prefer	prefiero, etc.
probar	to try	pruebo, etc.
querer	to wish / want	quiero, etc.
recordar	to remember	recuerdo, etc.
repetir	to repeat	repito, etc.
sentir	to feel	siento, etc.
sugerir	to suggest	sugiero, etc.
servir	to serve	sirvo, etc.
vestir	to wear	visto, etc.

Exercise 5

Complete the sentences with the appropriate form of the present tense of the verb in brackets.

1. ¿Vosotros .... viajar en coche o en tren? (preferir)

2. ¿Qué .... tú tomar? (querer)

3. Mis padres .... volver a Chile al final del verano. (pensar)

4. Yo .... ocho horas cada noche. (dormir)

5. ¿A qué hora .... las chicas? (volver)

6. Entre semana, mi hermano siempre .... muy temprano. (acostarse)

7. Nosotros .... direcciones en el centro de información turística. (pedir)

8. Al acabar las clases, los estudiantes .... en seguida. (marcharse)

9. Las joyas .... demasiado. (costar)

10. La tienda .... a las ocho. (cerrar)

Why not try to work out what each of these sentences means in English?

Irregular verbs

We have already seen that the verbs **'estar'** and **'ser'** are irregular in the present tense. A number of other common verbs are also irregular:

> No sé.
> *I don't know.*

> ¿Qué haces los fines de semana?
> *What do you do at the weekend?*

> Tengo 15 años.
> *I'm fifteen.*

Spanish has fewer irregular verbs than many other languages and here is a list of the most common ones. Verbs which are irregular are usually the ones which are most often used so there's really nothing else for it – you'll need to learn them! Luckily most of them are only irregular in the first person.

dar	singular	plural
1st	doy	damos
2nd	das	dais
3rd	da	dan

decir	singular	plural
1st	digo	decimos
2nd	dices	decís
3rd	dice	dicen

hacer	singular	plural
1st	hago	hacemos
2nd	haces	hacéis
3rd	hace	hacen

ir	singular	plural
1st	voy	vamos
2nd	vas	vais
3rd	va	van

saber	singular	plural
1st	sé	sabemos
2nd	sabes	sabéis
3rd	sabe	saben

salir	singular	plural
1st	salgo	salimos
2nd	sales	salís
3rd	sale	salen

tener	singular	plural
1st	tengo	tenemos
2nd	tienes	tenéis
3rd	tiene	tienen

venir	singular	plural
1st	vengo	venimos
2nd	vienes	venís
3rd	viene	vienen

Exercise 6

Complete the sentences with the appropriate form of the present tense of the verb in brackets.

1. Yo .... de casa cada mañana a las ocho. (salir)

2. Mi padre .... muchos viajes al extranjero. (hacer)

3. Nosotros no .... qué día es el último examen. (saber)

4. ¿Cuándo .... tú a vernos en España? (venir)

5. Los profesores siempre nos .... que hay que estudiar más. (decir)

The future tense

In many cases the idea of the future is conveyed in Spanish by the present tense:

> e.g.   Te veo mañana.
> *I'll see you tomorrow.*
>
> Vuelvo dentro de una hora.
> *I'll be back in an hour.*

or by the expression '**ir a**' followed by the infinitive:

e.g. Voy a comprar el anillo para mi mamá.
I'm going to buy the ring for my mother.

Vamos a ver la nueva película de Benicio del Toro.
We're going to see the new Benicio del Toro film.

When you do wish to use the **Future Tense** though, it is very straightforward. We have one set of endings for all verbs:

	singular	plural
1st	-é	-emos
2nd	-ás	-éis
3rd	-á	-án

Then we simply add our endings to the infinitive itself!

comprar	singular	plural
1st	compraré	compraremos
2nd	comprarás	compraréis
3rd	comprará	comprarán

comer	singular	plural
1st	comeré	comeremos
2nd	comerás	comeréis
3rd	comerá	comerán

vivir	singular	plural
1st	viviré	viviremos
2nd	vivirás	viviréis
3rd	vivirá	vivirán

You can see that the endings for all verbs are the same. Another good thing is that there are very few irregular verbs. All of these use the same endings as regular verbs and mostly, the only difference being that they either have a slightly shortened version of the infinitive or they are inserting a '**d**'.

The most common irregular futures are:

decir – diré	hacer – haré	poder – podré
poner – pondré	querer – querré	saber – sabré
salir – saldré	tener – tendré	valer – valdré
venir – vendré	hay – habrá	

The future tense is normally used for making promises, for provisional statements about the future and to express the idea of probability:

e.g. Viernes a las ocho nos veremos en la plaza.
We'll see each other in the square on Friday at eight o'clock.

¿Dónde está Marta? – Estará en el jardín.
Where is Marta? She's probably in the garden.

Si hay algún problema, te llamaré.
If there is any problem, I'll call you.

Exercise 7a

Complete the sentences with the appropriate form of the future of the verb in brackets.

1. ¿A qué hora .... la película? (ser)

2. Nosotros .... a Málaga el dos de octubre. (llegar)

3. Estoy seguro que tú .... la verdad. (decir)

4. Creo que los resultados de los exámenes .... en agosto. (salir)

5. Durante la visita, los chicos españoles .... a ver todos los monumentos históricos de Edimburgo. (ir)

Why not try to write down the English meaning of these sentences?

The conditional

There is another form of the verb which you have come across in a number of the set phrases in this book which is very similar to the future. It is called the Conditional and it is formed using the same stem as the future, but by changing the endings to:

	singular	plural
1st	-ía	-íamos
2nd	-ías	-íais
3rd	-ía	-ían

Pista

Make sure you learn these endings – they will come in useful for forming one of the past tenses!

So we have, for example,

Me gustaría ir a Málaga.
I would like to go to Malaga.

Sería interesante seguir estudiando español.
It would be interesting to carry on studying Spanish.

This form of the verb usually indicates what you would like to do or what would be the case, if it weren't for something else.

Exercise 7b

Complete the sentences as for Exercise 7a but this time use the appropriate part of the conditional.

The imperfect tense

Talking about the past in Spanish can seem like a problem for English speakers. This is because there are a number of different tenses used to do this. Let's take a look at the easiest of these first.

This is called the **imperfect tense** and is used to describe things in the past. It is formed as follows:

bailar	singular	plural
1st	bailaba	bailábamos
2nd	bailabas	bailábais
3rd	bailaba	bailaban

beber	singular	plural
1st	bebía	bebíamos
2nd	bebías	bebíais
3rd	bebía	bebían

vivir	singular	plural
1st	vivía	vivíamos
2nd	vivías	vivíais
3rd	vivía	vivían

Look at the endings of the '–er' and '–ir' verbs? Do they remind you of anything? If not, look back at the Conditional. That's right! These endings are the same as the endings for that form of the verb.

Only three verbs are irregular in this tense:

Ser	singular	plural
1st	era	éramos
2nd	eras	erais
3rd	era	eran

Ir	singular	plural
1st	iba	íbamos
2nd	ibas	ibais
3rd	iba	iban

ver	singular	plural
1st	veía	veíamos
2nd	veías	veíais
3rd	veía	veían

As we said before, this tense is used to describe things in the past, to say how things were, what they used to be like or what people **used to** think. For example:

Cuando tenías doce años ¿dónde vivías?
When you were twelve, where did you used to live?

Su padre era un hombre muy simpático.
His father was a very nice man.

Hace muchos años los europeos no sabían nada de América.
Many years ago, Europeans knew nothing about America.

Pista

The form 'hay' (there is, there are) is a special form of the verb 'haber', and in this tense it is 'había' (there was, there were).

Pista

Look out for 'trigger words' for the imperfect tense – always, every day/month/year, in the past, previously, when I was..., usually.

Exercise 8

Complete the sentences with the appropriate form of the imperfect of the verb in brackets.

1. ¿Qué tal .... el viaje a Londres? (estar)

2. Nosotros .... todas las noches en la fiesta. (bailar)

3. Todos los amigos .... siempre los mismos programas en la televisión. (ver)

4. La clase de historia .... muy interesante ayer. (ser)

5. Yo .... que no .... clase de español hoy. (pensar, tener)

The preterite (simple past) tense

The other very common past tense in Spanish is called the Preterite. This is generally used to talk about actions in the past (I went to the cinema, he fell down the stairs, she did her homework, etc.)

The endings for **regular verbs** are as follows:

–ar verbs	singular	plural
1st	-é	-amos
2nd	-aste	-asteis
3rd	-ó	-aron

–er and –ir verbs	singular	plural
1st	-í	-imos
2nd	-iste	-isteis
3rd	-ió	-ieron

For example:

bailar	singular	plural
1st	bailé	bailamos
2nd	bailaste	bailasteis
3rd	bailó	bailaron

beber	singular	plural
1st	bebí	bebimos
2nd	bebiste	bebisteis
3rd	bebió	bebieron

vivir	singular	plural
1st	viví	vivimos
2nd	viviste	vivisteis
3rd	vivió	vivieron

There are only four verbs which are completely irregular in this tense:

ir	singular	plural
1st	fui	fuimos
2nd	fuiste	fuisteis
3rd	fue	fueron

ser	singular	plural
1st	fui	fuimos
2nd	fuiste	fuisteis
3rd	fue	fueron

dar	singular	plural
1st	di	dimos
2nd	diste	disteis
3rd	dio	dieron

ver	singular	plural
1st	vi	vimos
2nd	viste	visteis
3rd	vio	vieron

You will note that '**ser**' and '**ir**' have the same forms in this tense. You will also note that '**dar**' and '**ver**' are only slightly irregular. '**Ver**' is only missing the written accents on the first and third persons singular and '**dar**' behaves like an '**er**' or '**ir**' verb, again without these same accents.

Some radical-changing '**ir**' verbs have changes in the third persons singular and plural in this tense. For example '**morir**' – to die, '**pedir**' – to ask and '**convertir**' – to convert

morir	singular	plural
1st	morí	morimos
2nd	moriste	moristeis
3rd	murió	murieron

pedir	singular	plural
1st	pedí	pedimos
2nd	pediste	pedisteis
3rd	pidió	pidieron

convertir	singular	plural
1st	convertí	convertimos
2nd	convertiste	convertisteis
3rd	convirtió	convirtieron

The other verbs which are irregular in this tense all follow the same pattern. In Spanish, this pattern has a special name – it is called **pretérito grave** – and for these forms you need a new set of endings. These are:

	singular	plural
1st	-e	-imos
2nd	-iste	-isteis
3rd	-o	-ieron

Then, you do have to learn the first person singular of each verb. That gives you a stem to add your endings on to. Be careful, though, some of these are tricky, as they can be quite different from the basic form of the verb.

Here are some of the most common ones:

andar – anduve

conducir – conduje (producir and reducir are like conducir)

decir – dije

estar – estuve

hacer – hice

poder – pude

poner – puse (componer, deponer and oponer are like poner)

querer – quise

saber – supe

tener – tuve (contener, detener, obtener and retener are like tener)

venir – vine

As we said before, this tense is used for talking about **actions** in the past, for saying what people did or what happened. For example,

Nací en el año 1989.
I was born in 1989.

Mi padre compró un nuevo coche ayer.
My father bought a new car yesterday.

Mi hermana aprobó todos sus exámenes el año pasado.
My sister passed all her exams last year.

Sometimes, you will find the **imperfect** and the **simple past** together. In those cases, the **imperfect** will be describing what was going on when something else happened; the **simple past** will be used for the thing that happened. For example:

Los chicos ponían la mesa cuando su madre llegó.
The children were laying the table when their mother arrived.

Llovía cuando llegamos al aeropuerto.
It was raining when we arrived at the airport.

Pista ⟩ Tip

- If you are not sure which tense to choose between **imperfect** and **simple past** try imagining that you are at the cinema, or the theatre or a football match. We've all been in situations like that and know what it is like to be looking at the main action and still be able to see other things in the background. Ask yourself the question: am I talking about the main action or something in the background? The main action will be **simple past** and the background, **imperfect**.

Exercise 9

Complete the sentences with the appropriate form of the simple past tense of the verb in brackets.

1. Mi clase .... un viaje a España. (hacer)

2. Los chicos estaban hablando cuando la profesora .... (entrar)

3. Nosotros .... todo en orden. (poner)

4. ¿ .... tú alguna especialidad mexicana durante las vacaciones? (comer)

5. El director me lo .... (decir)

6. De pequeño mi padre .... tres años en Irlanda. (vivir)

7. Todos .... que salir en seguida. (tener)

8. Su abuelo .... en la guerra. (morir)

9. ¿Quién te lo ....? (dar)

10. Vosotros .... el arroz a la cubana ¿verdad? (pedir)

Other past tenses – perfect and pluperfect

There are another two important past tenses which you may come across or wish to use, and these are fairly straightforward. The important thing to remember here is that these are **compound tenses** made up of more than one part.

The first part that you need for these tenses is either the present or the imperfect tenses of the verb '**haber**' (to have). These are:

Present	singular	plural
1st	he	hemos
2nd	has	habéis
3rd	ha	han

Imperfect	singular	plural
1st	había	habíamos
2nd	habías	habíais
3rd	había	habían

The second part you need is called the past participle to make these tenses. The past participle is formed like this for regular verbs:

> hablar – hablado
> vender – vendido
> vivir – vivido

and there are very few verbs which have an irregular form. The most important ones are:

> abrir – abierto
> cubrir – cubierto
> decir – dicho
> escribir – escrito
> hacer – hecho
> morir – muerto
> poner – puesto
> romper – roto
> ver – visto
> volver – vuelto

The present tense of '**haber**' is used to form the perfect and the imperfect to form the pluperfect. The main use of the **perfect tense** it to talk about something which '**has happened**'.

> ¿Has visitado España alguna vez?
> *Have you ever visited Spain?*

> Mi amiga aún no ha vuelto a casa.
> *My friend hasn't come home yet.*

Pista

This is a very useful part of the verb as you can also use it as an adjective, e.g. 'la ventana está rota'; 'unos ejercicios escritos', etc.

Pista

Look at the examples we have given. This tense often works just as it does in English, using a form of 'to have' followed by another part of the main verb.

Following on from this, the **pluperfect** is a very easy tense to use. It is used quite simply when you are talking about something which '**had happened**'.

> Cuando llegamos, la clase había empezado.
> *When we arrived, the class had started.*

> Los chicos mexicanos ya habían estudiado inglés en su tierra.
> *The Mexican boys had already studied English in their own country.*

Commands and the subjunctive

Another important way that we use verbs is to ask (or tell!) people to do things.

One way of doing this is to use the **conditional tense** of verbs like '**gustar**', '**querer**' or '**poder**'. For example:

> ¿Te gustaría venir al cine con nosotros?
> *Would you like to come to the cinema with us?*

> Vamos a jugar al fútbol. ¿Querrías acompañarnos?
> *We are going to play football. Would you like to come with us?*

> Estoy buscando mi boli. ¿Podrías ayudarme?
> *I'm looking for my pen. Could you help me?*

These are all quite polite ways of asking people to do things and, if we actually want to give them instructions, we have to learn two new forms of the verb: the command form (also called the imperative) and parts of something called the subjunctive. (You only need to know a few parts of this for the time being. If you go on to study Higher you will learn a lot more about it!)

The command form that you need to give instructions to someone you call '**tú**' is almost always the same as the **third person singular** form of the present tense. For example:

> ¡Habla con el profesor!
> *Talk to the teacher!*

> ¡Come tus verduras!
> *Eat your vegetables!*

> ¡Pide otro vaso de leche!
> *Ask for another glass of milk!*

There are only a very small number of verbs which have an irregular form for this type of instruction. Here are some examples of the most important ones:

decir – di: ¡Dime qué quieres!
              Tell me what you want!

hacer – haz: ¡Haz lo que te digo!
              Do what I tell you!

ir – ve: ¡Ve a la clase!
              Go to the class!

poner – pon: ¡Pon la mesa!
              Set the table!

| salir – sal: | ¡Sal al pasillo! |
| | *Go out into the corridor!* |

| tener – ten: | ¡Ten cuidado! |
| | *Be careful!* |

| ser – sé: | ¡Sé bueno! |
| | *Be good!* |

| venir – ven: | ¡Ven aquí! |
| | *Come here!* |

Giving instructions to more than one person is very easy. You only have to change the '**r**' at the end of the infinitive to '**d**' and you have the form you need for all verbs. For example:

¡Cantad *Flower of Scotland* para los estudiantes españoles!
Sing Flower of Scotland for the Spanish pupils!

¡Volved a casa temprano!
Come home early!

¡Escribid a vuestros padres!
Write to your parents!

There are no exceptions to this rule, you'll be glad to know!

For all other commands, for example, if you want to tell someone **not** to do something, or if you were going to call anyone '**usted**' and were going to tell them to do something, then you need to learn a new form of the verb called the **present subjunctive**.

To form the present subjunctive we take the **first person singular** of the present tense, take off the '**o**' and add endings which are very similar to the normal present tense. So our regular verbs will look like this:

hablar	singular	plural
1st	hable	hablemos
2nd	hables	habléis
3rd	hable	hablen

vender	singular	plural
1st	venda	vendamos
2nd	vendas	vendáis
3rd	venda	vendan

vivir	singular	plural
1st	viva	vivamos
2nd	vivas	viváis
3rd	viva	vivan

Can you see what we have done? Apart from the first person, we have put the endings from our '**–er**' verbs onto the '**–ar**' verbs, and we have put the endings from the '**–ar**' verbs onto the other two groups.

The radical changing verbs which we saw in the present tense have the same 'L' shaped pattern of changes as they had there. For example:

pensar	singular	plural
1st	piense	pensemos
2nd	pienses	penséis
3rd	piense	piensen

poder	singular	plural
1st	pueda	podamos
2nd	puedas	podáis
3rd	pueda	puedan

The only difference is that those '**–ir**' verbs, like '**pedir**' and '**seguir**', which change '**e**' to '**i**', keep their new vowel throughout this time. So we have, for example:

repetir	singular	plural
1st	repita	repitamos
2nd	repitas	repitáis
3rd	repita	repitan

Another slightly odd thing about '**–ir**' radical changing verbs in this form is that those like '**dormir**', where '**o**' changes to '**ue**', have a '**u**' instead of an '**o**' in the first and second person plural. For example:

morir	singular	plural
1st	muera	muramos
2nd	mueras	muráis
3rd	muera	mueran

The only verbs which are completely irregular in this form are those where the first person singular of the present tense doesn't end in '**o**'. The present subjunctive of these verbs is as follows:

dar	singular	plural
1st	dé	demos
2nd	des	deis
3rd	dé	den

estar	singular	plural
1st	esté	estemos
2nd	estés	estéis
3rd	esté	estén

haber	singular	plural
1st	haya	hayamos
2nd	hayas	hayáis
3rd	haya	hayan

ir	singular	plural
1st	vaya	vayamos
2nd	vayas	vayáis
3rd	vaya	vayan

saber	singular	plural
1st	sepa	sepamos
2nd	sepas	sepáis
3rd	sepa	sepan

ser	singular	plural
1st	sea	seamos
2nd	seas	seáis
3rd	sea	sean

So we will tell someone not to do something like this:

¡No me digas eso!
Don't tell me that!

¡No hables en la clase!
Don't talk in class!

¡No comas demasiados dulces!
Don't eat too many deserts!

¡No salgáis sin la llave!
Don't go out without the key!

¡No penséis en los exámenes el fin de semana!
Don't think about the exams at the weekend!

Or you will tell someone that you call '**usted**' to do something like this:

Perdóneme, señor, ¿dónde están los servicios?
Excuse me, sir, where are the toilets?

¡Siga todo recto!
Carry on straight ahead.

No ponga los libros en la mesa, por favor.
Don't put the books on the table please.

Pista) Tip

- There are lots of other uses of this form of the verb which you will study if you take your Spanish further, by going on to Higher, for example. In case you come across any of them before that – don't panic! They will normally have the same meaning as the present tense of the verb – although sometimes it will make more sense in English if you put another form like may/might/could/should/will before the main verb.

Exercise 10

Complete the sentences with the appropriate command form of the verb in brackets for someone that you call '**tú**'.

1. .... la primera calle a la derecha. (tomar)

2. .... todo recto hasta la segunda a la izquierda. (seguir)

3. No .... la esquina. (doblar).

4. .... allí la llegada del hornero. (esperar)

5. No .... a casa sin el pan. (volver)

Prepositions

Another group of very important words are called prepositions. These are used to show position and other similar relationships between words. It is important to be able to use these well in order to describe things or give directions

Here are some of the common of prepositions with some examples of how they are used:

a – *to/on/at*
Doy el libro a María.
I give the book to Maria.

El teatro está a la derecha.
The theatre is on the right.

Vende las naranjas a 2 euros el kilo.
He sells oranges at 2 Euros a kilo.

Pista **Tip**

- When '**a**' and '**de**' come directly before '**el**', then they are combined and written as one word, so that we have the forms '**al**' and '**del**'. For example '**Voy al cine**'. *I'm going to the cinema*, '**El aula está en la primera planta del colegio**'. *The classroom is on the first floor of the school.*

bajo – *under*
El niño se escondió bajo la escalera.
The child hid under the stairs.

con – *with*
Llegamos con sus primos.
We arrived with his cousins.

contra – *against*
La silla estaba apoyada contra la pared.
The chair was leaning against the wall.

de – *of/from*
Soy de Aberdeen.
I'm from Aberdeen.

Quisiera una taza de café.
I'd like a cup of coffee.

Pista **Tip**

- '**de**' can combine with other words to form what are called **compound prepositions**. These can be very useful when describing places or giving directions, and the most common ones are: '**al final de**' – *at the end of*; '**cerca de**' – *near to*; '**debajo de**' – *underneath*; '**delante de**' – *in front of*; '**dentro de**' – *inside of*; '**detrás de**' – *behind*; '**encima de**' – *on top of*; '**lejos de**' – *far from*.

desde – *from/since*
Estamos aquí desde ayer.
We have been here since yesterday

Nos enviaron una postal desde Benidorm.
They sent us a postcard from Benidorm.

entre – *between*	Los pirineos están situados entre Francia y España. *The Pyrenees are situated between France and Spain.*
hasta – *as far as/until*	Estuvieron allí desde marzo hasta mayo. *They were there from March until May.* Viajaron en autobús hasta Badajoz. *They travelled by bus as far as Badajoz.*
en – *in/into/on/at/by*	Madrid está en España. *Madrid is in Spain.* Entré en el colegio para buscar al profesor. *I went into the school to look for the teacher.* El libro está en la mesa. *The book is on the table.* Estudio ocho asignaturas en el colegio. *I study eight subjects at school.* Prefiero viajar en avión. *I prefer to travel by plane.*
por – *for/by*	Estábamos en Italia por un mes. *We were in Italy for a month.* Le llamaron por teléfono. *They called him by phone.*
para – *for/in order to*	El regalo es para mi madre. *The present is for my mother.* Estudio mucho para aprobar mis exámenes. *I study a lot in order to pass my exams.*
sin – *without*	Están sin trabajo. *They are without work.*
sobre – *on top of*	Los cuadernos estaban sobre la mesa. *The notebooks were on the table.*

Exercise 11

Make a note of these examples in your notebook. Leave plenty of room for others that you will come across during your Standard Grade course.

Constructions with the infinitive

The other main use of prepositions is to help you use two verbs together in a sentence, with the second one being an infinitive. It is very important to master this skill if you want to develop your Spanish really well.

Here are some of the most common verbs which combine with prepositions in this way, with an example of how each is used:

acabar de	Acabo de entregar mis deberes. *I have just handed in my homework.*
acabar por	Acabamos por volver a casa. *We ended up going home.*

acordarse de	Se acordaron de estudiar sus apuntes. *They remembered to study their notes.*
aprender a	Aprendíamos a tocar la guitarra. *We were learning to play the guitar.*
ayudar a	Nos ayudaron a encontrar nuestro hotel. *They helped us to find our hotel.*
dejar de	¿Dejaste de estudiar el francés? *Did you give up studying French?*
empezar a	Empiezo a creer que no están aquí. *I am beginning to believe that they are not here.*
empezar por	Empezamos por poner la mesa. *We began by setting the table.*
estar para	Estoy para salir. *I'm about to go out.*
insistir en	Insistieron en acompañarnos. *They insisted on coming with us.*
invitar a	Me invitó a cenar con sus padres. *She invited me to dinner with her parents.*
ir a	Voy a comprar el anillo para mi madre. *I'm going to buy the ring for my mother.*
pensar en	Pienso en estudiar alemán en la universidad. *I'm thinking about studying German at university.*
ponerse a	Se pusieron a llorar. *They started to cry.*
prepararse a	Nos preparamos a celebrar su cumpleaños. *We prepared to celebrate her birthday.*
quedar en	Quedamos en encontrarnos a las ocho en la plaza. *We agreed to meet at eight o'clock in the square.*
quedar por	Muchas cosas quedan por hacer. *There are lots of things still to do.*
soñar con	Sueño con ganar la lotería nacional. *I dream of winning the national lottery.*
tratar de	Tratamos de estudiar más. *We are trying to study more.*
volver a	Volvimos a ver *El señor de los anillos*. *We saw Lord of the Rings again.*

Being able to combine two verbs in the same sentence like this will make your Spanish much more impressive. In addition to these verbs which use a preposition, there are a small number which can be followed directly by another verb.

Here are the some of the most common of these, with an example of how they are used:

conseguir	Conseguí comprar billetes para el concierto. *I managed to buy tickets for the concert.*

deber	Deberíamos estudiar más. *We should study more.*
decidir	Decidieron quedarse en casa. *They decided to stay at home.*
esperar	Esperan aprobar sus exámenes. *They hope to pass their exams.*
evitar	No evitaron ver al abuelo. *They couldn't avoid seeing their grandfather.*
lograr	Logré encontrar un buen asiento en el estadio. *I managed to find a good seat in the stadium.*
necesitar	Necesitamos tener más dinero para las vacaciones. *We must have more money for the holidays.*
olvidar	Olvidó poner el libro en el bolso. *He forgot to put the book in his bag.*
parecer	Parecen considerarme como su hijo. *They seem to consider me as their son.*
pensar	Pienso quedarme otro año en el colegio. *I intend to stay on at school for another year.*
poder	Puedo ayudarte si quieres. *I can help you if you wish.*
preferir	Prefieren gastar su dinero en videojuegos. *They prefer to spend their money on computer games.*
prometer	Prometemos pasar más tiempo con los abuelos. *We promise to spend more time with our grandparents.*
querer	¿Quieres tomar algo? *Do you want something to drink?*
saber	Mi padre sabe cocinar muy bien. *My father can (i.e. knows how to) cook very well.*
soler	Solemos pasar las vacaciones en las Islas Canarias. *We usually spend our holidays in the Canary Isles.*
Temer	Temen perder el inicio de la película. *They are afraid they'll miss the start of the film.*

In addition to all of these, there is one very important verb which links to others with 'que'. To say that we must do something, we use:

Tener	Tenemos que mejorar nuestro español. *We must improve our Spanish*

Exercise 12

Make a note of these examples in your notebook. Leave plenty of room for others that you will come across during your Standard Grade course. Mastering these will really help you to improve your Spanish!

Answer key to the grammar exercises

Exercise 1

1. La piscina está en un palacio <u>antiguo</u> en el centro de la ciudad.

2. El inglés es mi asignatura <u>favorita</u>.

3. No todos los profesores son <u>divertidos</u>.

4. Estos exámenes son <u>importantes</u>.

5. Mi hermana es muy <u>ágil</u>.

Exercise 2

1. <u>Ellos</u> son de España.

2. <u>Ella</u> está en mi clase.

3. <u>La</u> preparan antes de salir.

4. Victoria <u>los</u> pone en la mesa.

5. Jaime <u>lo</u> bebe.

6. <u>Les</u> ofrezco los billetes.

7. El profesor <u>le</u> explica el problema.

8. <u>Se lo</u> damos.

9. Los libros nuevos son para <u>ellos</u>.

10. Llamaron por <u>ella</u>.

Exercise 3

1. La profesora <u>habla</u> cuatro idiomas.

2. En Benidorm, nosotros siempre <u>comemos</u> en el mismo restaurante chino.

3. Los abuelos de mi compañero español <u>viven</u> cerca de Barcelona.

4. Durante las vacaciones, yo <u>nado</u> cada día en el mar.

5. ¿<u>Buscas</u> tú un intercambio con un chico escocés?

Exercise 4

1. Mi madre <u>es</u> de Venezuela.

2. Las fuentes <u>están</u> en la Plaza de España.

3. No podemos ir al colegio porque <u>estamos</u> resfriados.

4. La física <u>es</u> una asignatura difícil.

5. <u>Estoy</u> muy preocupado a causa de mis estudios.

Exercise 5

1. ¿Vosotros <u>preferís</u> viajar en coche o en tren?

2. ¿Qué <u>quieres</u> tú tomar?

3. Mis padres <u>piensan</u> volver a Chile al final del verano.

4. Yo <u>duermo</u> ocho horas cada noche.

5. ¿A qué hora <u>vuelven</u> las chicas?

6. Entre semana, mi hermano siempre <u>se acuesta</u> muy temprano.

7. Nosotros <u>pedimos</u> direcciones en el centro de información turística.

8. Al acabar las clases, los estudiantes <u>se marchan</u> en seguida.

9. Las joyas <u>cuestan</u> demasiado.

10. La tienda <u>cierra</u> a las ocho.

Exercise 6

1. Yo <u>salgo</u> de casa cada mañana a las ocho.

2. Mi padre <u>hace</u> muchos viajes al extranjero.

3. Nosotros no <u>sabemos</u> qué día es el último examen.

4. ¿Cuándo <u>vienes</u> tú a vernos en España?

5. Los profesores siempre nos <u>dicen</u> que hay que estudiar más.

Exercise 7a

1. ¿A qué hora <u>será</u> la película?

2. Nosotros <u>llegaremos</u> a Málaga el dos de octubre.

3. Estoy seguro que tú <u>dirás</u> la verdad.

4. Creo que los resultados de los exámenes <u>saldrán</u> en agosto.

5. Durante la visita, los chicos cspañoles <u>irán</u> a ver todos los monumentos históricos de Edimburgo.

Exercise 7b

1. ¿A qué hora <u>sería</u> la película

2. Nosotros <u>llegaríamos</u> a Málaga el dos de octubre

3. Estoy seguro que tú <u>dirías</u> la verdad.

4. Creo que los resultados de los exámenes <u>saldrían</u> en agosto.

5. Durante la visita, los chicos españoles <u>irían</u> a ver todos los monumentos históricos de Edimburgo.

Exercise 8

1. ¿Qué tal <u>estaba</u> el viaje a Londres?

2. Nosotros <u>bailábamos</u> todas las noches en la fiesta.

3. Todos los amigos <u>veían</u> siempre los mismos programas en la televisión.

4. La clase de historia <u>era</u> muy interestante ayer.

5. Yo <u>pensaba</u> que no <u>tenía</u> clase de español hoy.

Exercise 9

1. Mi clase <u>hizo</u> un viaje a España.

2. Los chicos estaban hablando cuando la profesora <u>entró</u>.

3. Nosotros <u>pusimos</u> todo en orden.

4. ¿<u>Comiste</u> tú alguna especialidad mexicana durante las vacaciones?

5. El director me lo <u>dijo</u>.

6. De pequeño mi padre <u>vivió</u> tres años en Irlanda.

7. Todos <u>tuvieron</u> que salir en seguida.

8. Su abuelo <u>murió</u> en la guerra.

9. ¿Quién te lo <u>dio</u>?

10. Vosotros <u>pedisteis</u> el arroz a la cubana ¿verdad?

Exercise 10

1. <u>Toma</u> la primera calle a la derecha.

2. <u>Sigue</u> todo recto hasta la segunda a la izquierda.

3. No <u>dobles</u> la esquina.

4. <u>Espera</u> allí la llegada del hornero.

5. No <u>vuelvas</u> a casa sin el pan.